Being With the Without

COVER: Roman civilization, 2nd century A.D. Asarotos oikos mosaic (unswept room), depicting a mouse feeding on food remains on the floor. Roman copy of Hellenistic original by Sosos of Pergamon. From Rome, Vigna Lupi. Vatican, Museo Gregoriano Profano.
© 2013. DeAgostini Picture Library/Scala, Florence.

English proof-reading: Peter Hanly.
French proof-reading: Jacques Mangold and Marcel Mangold.
Transcription: Soraya Guimarães Hoepfner.

We would like to thank the Foundation for Baltic and East European Studies, *Östersjöstiftelsen* (Sweden) for the economic support that made it possible for the project *Loss of Grounds as Common Ground* to visit Jean-Luc Nancy in Strasbourg and to produce this book which became the outcome of the discussions.

© Copyright the Authors and Axl Books, 2013.

Axl Books, Stockholm, 2013
www.axlbooks.com
info@axlbooks.com

ISBN 978-91-86883-18-8

Being With the Without

Marcia Sá Cavalcante Schuback
Jean-Luc Nancy
(eds.)

Contents

Preface	vii
FIRST DAY: AT THE UNIVERSITY	
Introduction	1
Beings-with after 1989: Stolen communities?	4
The Story of «Co-», or What has Been Forgotten in the History of Being Together (From the General Equivalence of Money to the Un-equivalence of Every Singular Being)	11
On Brackets and on Being a Marxist-In-A-Certain-Sense (An Engineered Community: Liberty and Equality without Brotherhood?)	20
For Freedom, Against Emancipation. Fraternity, Paternity, Sensibility (Marx' Narrow Field of Vision)	27
Alienation: «How Much Heimat does One Need?»	32
«Dass uns erst im Verlust des Verlorenen aufscheint, was uns gehört» or Presence vs. Tension (How to Think Sensibility and Desire?)	34
One that is Bigger than Subject: «Chaque fois unique, la fin du monde», or, God's Desire: «Cannot Not Do»	36
Myth with Plato, Mythos with Platonov, or, is Literature Sacrifice?	42
L'être sans comme fond sans fond de l'être avec (Being-Without as the Ground Without Ground of Being-With)	51
SECOND DAY: AT NANCY'S HOME	59
POST SCRIPTUM	
Absence: un hommage à Jean-Luc Nancy	97
Afterword	100
TRANSLATIONS	
To page 51ff.	103
To page 56ff.	107
To page 59ff.	109
To page 68ff.	110
To page 74ff.	115
To page 79ff.	116
To page 97ff.	118
To page 100	120

Preface

April 2012, a group from Sweden, consisting in philosophers, scholars of cultural studies, of intellectual history, of Russian Language and Literature, and of political science, came to Strasbourg to meet Jean-Luc Nancy and discuss the relation between being-with and being-without. Two seminars were held, the first of which took place at the University of Strasbourg. Jacob Rogozinski, Edouard Mehl and some doctoral students from the university were also present. The second seminar took place at Jean-Luc Nancy's home. Both seminars were recorded but some parts were lost due to technical problems during the recording. The present text is a reconstruction of what remained of the recordings, with some changes brought about by the work of memory and by the necessity of transposing spoken language into a written and readable one. This reconstruction can be read as a kind of mosaic made with pieces left over, with remnants. Sosos, the most famous mosaicist of Antiquity, developed a principle for his mosaics based on the remains left on the ground following a symposium, the *asárotos oikos*, (la maison non balayée, the un-swept home). He substituted the remains of food and other leftovers for the tesselations, the mosaic pieces, keeping the positions that chance selected for the remains of the party. This kind of decoration was called rhopography, a writing that gathers together a few little things – small remains and insignificant pieces that, when patiently put together by separating one from the other with a grey mortar, makes it possible for each mosaic piece, each *tessellae musivae*, to refract its own light. The seminar was held mostly in English but at certain moments French took over for some time. We have maintained this alternation of languages, and translated the French parts in the footnotes. The main topic for the discussion was being-without, the sense of absence and loss of grounds, discussed in tension with and in relation to ontological and sociopolitical-literary dimensions of «being-with». The «without» can be seen as the grey mortar that binds together and separates the small contributions of each participant. Because the mosaic work was done some months after the visit, small pieces, short passages, and brief observations continued to fall on the ground, remaining as tessellations to be brought together with the first ones. Peter Schuback recollected a small piece called *Absences,* written some years before, and dedicated it to Jean-Luc Nancy.

Marcia Sá Cavalcante Schuback

First Day:
At the University

Introduction

MARCIA SÁ CAVALCANTE SCHUBACK: On behalf of this small group that has come from Sweden to talk with you and to listen to you, I would like to thank you for receiving us, and also to thank Jacob Rogozinski and Edouard Mehl for offering this space at the university of Strasbourg for this first meeting. We come from Sweden, but at the same time we do not really come *from* Sweden, because we have different backgrounds and mother tongues – not only Swedish but also Portuguese from Brazil, Russian, Polish and German – and from different disciplines: philosophy, cultural studies, Slavic languages and literatures, and intellectual history. Rather than using the bureaucratic jargon of multiculturalism and multidisciplinarity, I would prefer to say that we are a group speaking and thinking in very different accents. What is common to this small group is that we have a research project focused around the question of «the loss of grounds as common ground». With our origins in different «disciplines» or, better said, in different theoretical cultures and traditions, each one of us has confronted your thinking on being-with through different discursive filters and in different manners. We come here, gratefully accepting – at least as I understood it from our email exchange and considering that the original intention was, on the contrary, to bring you to Sweden – your suggestion to be your guests. In this short introduction, speaking on behalf of our group (I am using «I» to mean «we»), I want to say that we were happy to receive your invitation «to come» as we are, without an agenda, or an already formulated discourse, or any formulas related to a definite school, or anything like that. That means that we have brought no doxa with us, whether orthodoxy or heterodoxy. Or maybe I should put it like this: we come here with a «without», for what is common to all of our different questions is a focus on the «loss» of grounds, the «without»- grounds, or the «without» of grounds. «No ground, say ground, no ground»: these words by Beckett would be a way to describe our arriving here with the without in our luggage. Our questions are related to, and depart from, the tension between your being-with and our being-without. Not nothing, but without. That is why our starting point is not connected with issues of creation and its nothingness, but with without-ness, so to speak.

Representing the research project «Loss of Grounds as Common Ground» are Ludger Hagedorn (Philosophy), Tora Lane (Russian Language and Literature), Leonard

INTRODUCTION

Neuger (Polish Language and Literature, although Leonard, unfortunately, could not be with us on this trip), Irina Sandomirskaja (Cultural Studies), Gustav Strandberg (Philosophy), and myself, Marcia Sá Cavalcante Schuback (Philosophy). Victoria Fareld (Intellectual History), Marcel Mangold (Political Science, and the translator of your *La vérité de la démocratie* for the forthcoming Swedish edition), Heinke Fabritius (Art History), Krystof Kasprzak (Philosophy) and Soraya Guimarães Hoepfner (Philosophy) are not officially part of the research project but are part of the group. With us also is Peter Schuback, a Swedish cellist and composer[1]. Some of us prepared some questions to discuss with you concerning the tension between with and without. Shall we proceed in a traditional way, with questions addressed to you and answers from you? A traditional way, but also non-traditional, insofar as we would all remain open to receiving a thought that may occur in-between thoughts, in the coming and going of questions and answers. Et en plus, on mélange les langues?, on laisse l'entre les langues, et entre le comprendre et pas comprendre devenir l'accent de cette rencontre?[2]

1. Doctoral students in the Department of Philosophy at the University of Strasbourg were also present, but unfortunately their questions at the end of this first day were not recorded because of technical problems with the recorder.
2. And further still, we might mix languages? We might allow the *between* of languages, and the between of comprehension and incomprehension to become the accent/tone/tonality of this encounter?

JEAN-LUC NANCY:³ Peut-être n'y a-t-il pas vraiment une opposition entre «traditionnel» et «non-traditionnel»: la tradition c'est aussi celle de l'échange, du frottement des cervelles, des esprits, des langages. Il s'agit moins de parler du «dialogue» dans sa figure heuristique et dialectique que plus simplement, plus humblement, des contacts, frottements, petits et grands chocs dans le magma desquels toujours «ça pense»: non des sujets pensent, mais l'époque, le monde pensent...

Beings-with after 1989: Stolen Communities?

IRINA SANDOMIRSKAJA: Our «without» arises in discussion with you, Professor Nancy, and is suggested by your concept of «being-with». I would like to ask you some questions about your book *Being Singular Plural*. This text was first published in 1996 and has, I believe, an important historical context that has to be taken into account. The way I see it, this book is inseparable from the 1990s (which began with the fall

---

3. Perhaps there is not really an opposition between «traditional» and «non-traditional»: tradition is also that of exchange, of frictions of minds, of sensibilities, of languages. It is less a question of «dialogue» in its heuristic and dialectic sense, than – more simply, more humbly – of contact, of frictions, of small and large shocks in the magma within which, always, «thought happens»: not of subjects that think, but the epoch, the world think...

of the Berlin Wall in 1989), and – tell me if I am mistaken – its concept is probably generated by the political and intellectual debate about the past, present, and future of Europe. In saying this, I am aware that I am probably narrowing down your intention of producing an ontology of being-with as community in reading into it a historical-political context. Still, as someone who deals with Russian and East European cultural history, rather than philosophy, and given also the centrality of the questions of community after the fall of communist regimes and during the period of so-called Europeanization, it is easier for me to understand your reasoning if I consider your writing against the background of the European thinking of the time; in which, I think, the idea itself of questioning community, and of looking for a new formula, is deeply rooted. The reason I am mentioning (the so-called) Europeanization is because I am afraid that the post-Wall European intellectual and political search for new communalities (commonalities) beyond nations and blocs is now over. I thought that it was highly symbolic this time I came to Berlin that the first word I read when I entered the arrival hall, was *Heimat*. Then I noticed that *Heimat* was now everywhere in the public language; and this was for me, sadly, another sign that the project of a post-communist Europe in the 1990s, with its well-intentioned but never achieved innovative being-withs, was now over.

What I find in *Being Singular Plural* is a way of thinking togetherness at the point where other historical forms of togetherness expose their non-viability. Such is the togetherness of a national state based on the fiction of a unitary origin. Such is also the togetherness of an empire, *E pluribus unum*[4], one out of many. Here, the plural is not important in itself, it is merely a transition to unity, the totality of the one. Equally exploitative and unjust, as we could see, was the proclaimed plurality of the communist regime, which was supposed to be – to quote Stalin – plural/«national» in terms of form but strictly unitary in terms of the communist content. In spite of the syntactic difference, this formula is as imperialist (as Walter Benjamin noticed as early as 1927) as the former one. Nevertheless, the loss of the «world socialist system» in 1989, even though its paradigm of community was deeply imperialist, still profoundly affected all liberal thinking, because it seemed then that along with it the general idea of any commonality at all was also lost. We remember that the USSR ultimately succumbed to the new liberalism of Reagan and Thatcher, which proclaimed society inexistent, which also produced the unbridled rule of neoliberal imagination in East European states whose socialist economies were hastily and cruelly dismantled – one can actually say more rudely: stolen.

4. This expression, found in Cicero's *Pro Luentio*, 7, 22, in Ovid's *Tristia* 1, 3, 16 and also in Menander's *Samia*, received a variant meaning when used as a motto for the American federation, signifying then togetherness makes the force, builds strengh. The formula is the motto on USA's coat of arms and also the song of Latin American *guerrileros*, «el pueblo unido jamás sera vencido», see the work of the American composer Fredric Rzewski *The people united will never be defeated* (http://www.youtube.com/watch?v=h6-MhlBSBrM&noredirect=1)

Meanwhile, in *Being Singular Plural*, everything appears prefixed with a «co-«, or a «mit-», a «miteinander-», a «with». Being is not just prefixed, but reversed: as a first philosophy, Being-with is postulated to be anterior to Being as such. Thus, all existence is primarily coexistence, all appearing is co-appearing, all origins are co-origins, and all these formulas derive from a thesis about the anteriority of Being-With.

Two other principles are «the world is us» and «being is communication». It is these two on which I would like you to comment because, I am afraid, to my ears, used to the rhetorics of Europeanization, if you forgive me for saying so, they ring with overtones of European bureaucracy. I have a feeling that rather than describing relations between people they describe the principles of institutionalization. It is institutions who have the right to proudly say «meaning is us» (as Bruno Latour shows us in discovering that the institution and the narrative of the institution are the same thing). Institution produces and reproduces itself in self-communication. For an institution (but not for a human being, I believe), being is indeed communication, which reminds me of the situation in Kafka's «Castle» where all being amounts to a waiting for, a receiving or not receiving, a promising or an avoiding, a sending or intercepting, the delivering or misdelivering of a message. Because – it would seem – «meaning is us».

I am sure this was not at all your meaning but I would like to ask you to make some comments on your use of these words that have been so deeply corrupted by empty bureaucratic speech, especially since 1989 – and maybe purify them a little.

It sounds as if I am here repeating the critique that Herder, in his Essay on the *Origin of Language*[5], directed against the rationalism of Condillac and Rousseau, who described language as the product of human nature, alternatively as a result of a contract between men. In other words, in their own ways they also proclaimed that «meaning is us» and nothing else, implying by «us» the community of men as arbitrary sense makers. We remember that Herder presupposed a non-commensurability between man and his world. It is not that Herder opposed human finiteness to the infinity of the human world. The human world in Herder, just as in Jean-Luc Nancy, is as finite as the human himself. However, as distinct from other animals, humans have been given a world that is too big for them. As distinct from an insect that controls his world fully, the human has a span of attention too narrow to master the vast expanses he was given to live in. Hence, the necessity of language for man «to collect himself in a moment of wakefulness», as Herder puts it.[6] And hence, also, the importance

---

5. Johann Gottfried Herder. *Abhandlung über den Ursprung der Sprache*: Text, Materialien, Kommentar / Wolfgang Pross, Carl Hanser, 1978
6. Johann Gottfried Herder, «Essay on the Origin of Language». Transl. by Alexander Gode. In: Moran, John H., Gode, Alexander (red), Rousseau, Jean-Jacques & Herder, Johann Gottfried von , *On the origin of language*, Univ. of Chicago Press, Chicago, 1986, p 116.

of language as appropriating this world, but not necessarily in such an exhaustive way as to completely reduce the meaning to the world to the human, to an «us». When I am speaking about the dangers of the word «communication» I am thinking about Walter Benjamin's warning against the proliferation of «communication» (in his understanding, a language driven by will to power) at the expense of the other fundamental principle of language, that of expression, or «*die Sprache überhaupt*», when things communicate themselves addressing a higher level of their existence. This is the danger he observes in the 1920s Moscow as he watches the language of revolution among the leftist intelligentsia empoverishing and shrinking to institutional power talk. *Geschwätz*, as Benjamin called it using a term from Kierkegaard, referring to the latter's thesis about the degeneration of speech into prattle, i. e. into pure communication, in the absence of revolution. Most probably I have misunderstood your use of the word communication, and would like you to comment on this.

My other question concerns the «we». Emile Benveniste tells us that semantically, «we» has quite an unusual structure. Formally, it represents the plural of the first person. However, as compared to other plural forms, like boys, girls, men, or women, «we» is different. «Boys» means one boy, and another, and another, and so on. But «we» does not mean an I, and another I, and so on. «*Vous*» is the plural of «*tu*» because it means «tu and tu». But «we» can mean either «you and me» (as opposed to them) or «me and them» (as opposed to you), but not «I and I». In the meantime, it seems to me that you are using this «we» precisely to denote a plurality of «I»s, a plurality of singularities: «all the dead and the living and all beings», as you put it. So, what is this «us» that does not have a «them» to complement or to oppose it? You are saying:

> we have to dis-identify ourselves *from* every sort of «we» that would be the subject of its own representation»... «we» is not representational but a praxis anterior to every thought.[7]

Such a «we» as constituted by the relations of «with» – «neither mediate or immediate», «the closeness, the brushing up against or the coming across, the almost there of distanced proximity»; such a «we» that is only constituted by its space and maybe also by the chance of «coming across» – how can it be a ground for an ethics?

So, to return. Your thesis is that such a «we» coincides with meaning: «meaning is us». This thesis is viable only as long as we preserve the first thesis, namely, that all being is communication. Would not this reduce meaning to pure communication, a situation whose dangers Benjamin

---

7. Jean-Luc Nancy. *Being Singular Plural*, (California: Stanford University Press, 2000), p. 71 (translation modified)

warned us of? From Benjamin's point of view, such a reduction would mean a flattening, the elimination of depth and height, the vertical dimension of making sense. I am sure you did not mean anything like that, but, as I already said, the polysemantic words of the formulas appear to me corrupted by other uses, and I would like to ask you to clarify your meaning. I am sure I haven't got the point, and I ask you to forgive me for that, but this is what I think I am reading in(to) your book.

The Story of «Co-» or What has Been Forgotten in the History of Being Together (From the General Equivalence of Money to the Un-equivalence of Every Singular Being)

JLN: Oh thank you, certainly you've got everything. You know, a book is a strange thing, you take a book by Platonov or Nancy and you think that it looks like a kind of bible. I read it and I get the feeling, or imagination, or *phantasma* that everything in the book would be conceived of, prepared and exhibited in absolutely the right way, by that supposed *Author* that we have in mind. Every person that writes knows that this is not the case. The book is open to the reader and the reader rewrites the book. All your questions are right and show me how much there is to be done to go further, and in so many directions.

But first, let me answer the question about the relationship between the book in 1996 and the status of Europe at that time. Two things can be said. On the one hand, you are right. If I remember well, on the first pages of the book there is a report about all the wars that were going on. It was the time of the Balkan war, and the book attests to its historical context. On the other hand, you said briefly «I know you are speaking at the level of ontology, but...» But what? What does it mean, ontology?

The main question for me was the question of community, of being-with. At that time, it became the question of the singular and the plural, which had itself begun some years earlier, in a book from 1986, *The Inoperative Community*. All this has been about the word «common» – or, as you say, about the «co» – which at the same time is very special because it marks the word «communism», that played such a role in the more than two centuries of our history following the word's first appearance at the end of the 18th century. Here, ontology means – I would say in parallel with Heidegger – what has been forgotten in the history of being together. Even if it is a partly formal parallel to make things clear, we could say that this «together», togetherness, the «co» was forgotten in the history of the word «communism». The word communism makes its appearance at the end of the 18th century and it was so important for the 19th century until precisely the time when it began to deteriorate, to become desiccated.

THE STORY OF «CO-»

I think there is a reason for that, something coming from the beginning of our Western history, namely, the foundation of the *polis*. What does the *polis* mean? I would say that the *polis* is the name of the first togetherness in which no common ground of being together is given. Before the *polis*, there were different kinds of being together: the rural, or agricultural community, or what Marx described as the archaic community, or other ways of being together within empires. But those empires did not constitute any *E pluribus unum*. I think that for the pharaoh of Egypt or the king of Babylon, there existed no *E pluribus unum*, but only imperial power and order under which every small community was able to live its own life.

With the *polis*, the empire departs and communities set up by the gods separate. That was the beginning of something absolutely new which, just as we are nowadays, were together without any given ground. It meant also the invention by men of the ground that takes the name of the law. The invention of the law – and the ground – is *isonomia*. This invention did not depend on the idea of equality. On the contrary, equality was produced by the necessity to invent law and to construct togetherness on this absolutely new ground. But then the story becomes quite complicated because at the starting point of the *polis*, whether the Greek or the Roman one, there was a peculiar civil religion, or something we can call a civil religion. Indeed, what is the origin of philosophy if not the condemnation of Socrates who was sentenced for not paying attention to the gods of the city?

And we know that later, too, at the moment of another attempt to found a new *polis*, or a new democracy, there was an appeal to a civil religion. What does it mean? In a certain way, even though I won't be able to relate the whole story here, the question of civil religion means that, maybe, from Rome to Rousseau – that is, up until the Europe of the time of political and industrial revolution (because both take place together) – something was lost. What was lost is something that is given through religion but is not religion, something that Rousseau called in the chapter on civil religion, a «*rendre sensible au coeur du citoyen*», «making sensible to the heart of the citizen»[8] all the apparatuses of institutions, laws, and government. What was lost was sensibility.

Going very fast, I would say, then, that the first point in the «co» is sensibility, i.e., how we can feel being together. How can we find that feeling of being together – that in principle is supposed to be found only in religious community, or in a community of love – also in a civil community and later in communism (the historical, the so-called real communism)? It seems that the second step towards forgetting the core of the «co» was made under a communism that had little sensibility. Of course Mayakovsky, as a figure, seems to contradict this statement; but why did he (and of course many other people, too) have such a fate, if in early communism the question of

---

8. Jean-Jacques Rousseau, »Du Contrat Social ou Principes du Droit Politique» in *Oeuvres Complètes* (Pais: Furne et Cie, Librairies-Éditeurs, 1852)

free love and that of disturbing the social familial bourgeois order was so important, and why were they so quickly forgotten?

You know, Lenin's question «What is to be done?»[9], first appears in the title of the novel by Chernyshevsky. As a matter of fact, it was not a question, not an appeal, but the entire book is the answer to the question, and the answer is very important, it is the way to live as a «we». I do not remember if it is two men and one woman, or two women and one man, but simply that this is a new way of love, of sensibility. Of course, when Lenin quotes Chernyshevsky's novel, he is not interested in the story but uses the title because the novel was so popular despite the virulent critique by Tolstoy and Dostoevsky.

So, this will be my answer at this point. To sum up, I would say that the first content of the «co» is something that comes before and after any law, or any relationship if relationship is understood as a kind of technical or intellectual link. I would even add that sensibility of the mutual, of the common, is more than a link. Today everybody speaks about a social link, but a link is like a string that is not really visible. We say that friendship or love produces links but at the same time we are ready to agree that friendship or love are not exactly links, but something else. For example, we could say as a simple opposition, not a link but a touching. In the touching, there is no link, there is proximity but no

---

9. Vladimir Ilyich Lenin. *What is to be done? Burning questions of our movement* (1901-1902) http://marxists.org/archive/lenin/works/1901/witbd/index.htm

link. The link belongs to *fascio, faisceau*[10], as in «fascism» – and, as we know, in fascism the link is very important.

Well, then...did I succeed with my book – in doing what? In resisting the «*E pluribus unum*»? Of course not, absolutely not, and this was not the role the book was intended to play. The book is not a political action. Today, communitarianism produced by nationalism, or that produced by small communities that are not exactly nationalist, or the communitarian way of presenting the small group is much more important. Why? Because the time between the writing of the book and now – it is almost twenty years – has been dominated by what I would call the «anti-co» existence of capitalism. But capitalism is already an old word: we [should] call it extreme capitalism – financial capitalism.

Recently I discovered what the word *finance* means. Its etymology comes from *final*, that is, to make an end in some action or operation. And the end is to pay. I pay you, or you pay me, so that the whole relationship is finished.[11] And even

---

10. Italian for group, association, French lit. bundle.
11. Cf. finance (n.) finance at Dictionary.com c.1400, «an end, settlement, retribution,» from M.Fr. finance «ending, settlement of a debt» (13c.), noun of action from finer «to end, settle a dispute or debt,» from fin (see fine (n.)). Cf. M.L. finis «a payment in settlement, fine or tax.» The notion is of «ending» (by satisfying) something that is due (cf. Gk. telos «end;» pl. tele «services due, dues exacted by the state, financial means.» The French senses gradually were brought into English: «ransom» (mid-15c.), «taxation» (late 15c.); the sense of «management of money» first recorded in English 1770.

more interesting is that in French, at least according to Robert's historical Dictionary, it means «to pay or to make the other pay». Thus, financial capitalism is extreme capitalism not because, as one often hears today, it is some kind of excess of capitalism. The idea is that today's capitalism is «too much,» and that we have to control it and return to «good» capitalism. But there is no good capitalism, for many reasons, but also because capitalism represents the whole extent of the «non-co», the non-sensibility of togetherness, and the replacement of togetherness, of the «co», by Marx' «general equivalence», money. Money is nothing wrong in itself, except that it reduces everything to the same value: you can pay me or I can make you pay me. Thus I believe, we live at a time of the big destruction of the «co», and, for that reason, the time of a kind of insurrection of the «co» itself in communitarian and other forms.

I would like to take a step further as compared to this book. The question is not whether I, or anybody, succeed, but if we are able to think of a revolution. I do not mean a revolution to achieve a better society and better institutions, but a revolution of sensibility. Such a revolution is exactly what happened in early capitalism. Capitalism did not come from nowhere (or maybe, in a way, it came from nowhere), because that was the time when the whole of Europe (and at that time it was already Europe in the present-day sense of the word) was connected through communication and exchange between languages, quasi-nationalities, and religions. It was at that time that Europe invented credit and fiduciary money whose value was supposed to be based on confidence. This new money is all that we know as money, no longer gold or any other precious matter, but a symbol and representation in which we all have confidence.

This invention came from somewhere, but we are unable to say what it was, definitely not the ugly early capitalism making its first primitive accumulation. What was the reason that capitalism came into existence? The entire civilization started inventing a new kind of sensibility. Today, we can only ask if there is any possibility of grasping another kind of sensibility of exchange, that is, at least, another kind of non-equivalence, an in-equality which would not contradict the equality of beings (at least of human beings) but [would rather] act in favor of that equality; which would mean each being's absolute un-equivalence.

I think at this point I cannot but be Marxist. Marx says that every worker becomes work force and can be paid for that and become a commodity himself like other workers. Marx is absolutely right and we are more and more within that context, ambience, atmosphere, and sensibility. I have heard some Chinese people nowadays say: «We will become the master of the world, but if we are clever, we should not desire to become the master of the world in the same way as, say, the Americans. Can we do something that would originate in the Chinese tradition, invent another way?» Maybe it is an absolute contradiction; maybe if there is a ‹master of the world› you cannot be this in a non-conformist way. But for me that was a sign because it shows that for the Chinese people it is no longer as simple as merely saying «we will become the strongest». This latter was characteristic of Stalinism: the purpose of construction of the USSR was to become the master of the world like the Americans.

Then there is still the enormous question about communication in Kafka and communication and expression in Benjamin. I was surprised when you said that Kafka's *Castle* is a world of communication. Maybe the question is how to understand communication. If I wrote, «being is communication», then by communication I mean every way of being together. It is not communication of signification but communication of the senses, communication through art and friendship, love, proximity, and intimacy. What is intimacy, what does intimacy mean?

I try to think closer to Benjamin's notion of expression. Here another question is at stake, that of being in common, in which the earth is not only «the one» of the human being but also «the one» of everything. And then it becomes the question about the whole of creation. The starting point for me now is not from earth, not the direction that begins from what is supposed to be the human community towards the rest of the world. On the contrary, if there is a world, this means that several things are together, just that, nothing more. The big bang, before the big bang, there is no before, for you need more than one. The one as in *E pluribus unum* was, from the starting point, it was never the one. If it would have been the one, it would have destroyed itself. Hegel says that the one is its own negation; the one means several things, more than one, and maybe more than two because two makes a «we» even if it is only the relation between the two.

And if we discover now that we belong to the world and that there is nothing outside the world (you asked about the possibility of living outside the earth: it depends on what you mean by the earth. Outside of the earth as we know it, the earth of the humanity, outside of humanity – it is certainly possible. But outside of the world? No). And here begins the question about *nihil*, about nothing. There is nothing out of the world, no thing. Or maybe there is ‹not-something›, maybe there is an opening onto the world, towards nothing, but there is nothing out of the world.

On Brackets and on Being a Marxist-In-A-Certain-Sense (An Engineered Community: Liberty and Equality without Brotherhood?)

LUDGER HAGEDORN: Professor Nancy, an outstanding and famous title of one of your works is *La Communauté désœuvrée*. It was translated into English as «The Inoperative community», but maybe it could be rephrased as «The Undesigned Community»?

JLN: Undesigned?

LH: Yes, a community that has not been designed, where no design is being made.

JLN: Very good.

LH: Just a little remark at the beginning about our little inoperative community here: It looks, as if our talk has also been designed beforehand, because you already referred to Marx; and you said that you are a Marxist, in a certain sense. Now, my question is *about* Marx. Professor Nancy, sometimes you put a list of things into little inapparent brackets that are not so innocent as the brackets seem to indicate, for example the triad *communio, communism, communitarianism*. And in even just mentioning these words, which all relate to the co-, to the togetherness, we see that this triad unites and brings together realities that at first instance seem to be very far apart. If we asked e.g. a representative of the church, or someone with a theological background, what they have to do with communism, their answer might be: nothing at all. And the same would also hold for communitarianism. You mention especially one kind of communitarianism and you have called it nationalism, but certainly there is a variation of what is understood as communitarian. What I am thinking of is especially the contemporary American philosophical debate. And the reason why I really appreciate your brackets, is simply because they tell us that all these attempts have something in common. And even if the communitarians might not want to admit it, these brackets tell us for example that knowingly or unknowingly, willingly or unwillingly their approach shares something with communism and with *communio*, perhaps, and that there is a certain common background. This very nicely opens up a space in which to think about togetherness and the notion of community.

Against this background, I would like to refer to an early writing of Karl Marx, entitled «On the Jewish Question»[12]. It is a famous piece of writing, and also infamous because of some anti-Semitic undertones. Leaving this aside, I would like to point out two important characterizations that he gives here. The writing focuses on emancipation, first and foremost on emancipation from religion. The title seems to speak about emancipation from the Jewish religion only, but certainly Marx means emancipation from *any* religion. And even more, it is about human emancipation in general – a certain understanding of human emancipation at which he wants to arrive. Knowing that it is Marx who speaks, we can already guess what human emancipation means, namely that he wants to tackle a social question.

12. Karl Marx, «On the Jewish Question» (German original in *Deutsch-Französische Jahrbücher* in1844), in Karl Marx, *Selected Writings*, ed. Lawrence H. Simon, (Hackett: Indianapolis, 1994), pp. 1–26.

In one sense we can say that this article is very much the document of an enlightened, liberating move of human emancipation – emancipation from the constraints of religion, the constraints of tradition, the constraints of political serfdom and economic dependency. All this is very much in the sense of the Enlightenment. And Marx says: we do not only want political emancipation, but we want *human* emancipation, human emancipation is the important thing. Well, who would not shout out: «Yes»! Certainly we want human emancipation, but then the question is what that means. And what did human emancipation mean to Marx at that point? Looking at it, we see that for him it meant overcoming distinctions, as I would say. He speaks about the distinction between the bourgeois and the citizen, the *citoyen*. So there is one role that we play as political human beings and another one that we play as civil human being.

Coming back to the starting point – Marx asks about the role of religion and to him, certainly, it shouldn't have any role at all. And in this sense he then says: the distinction between the Jew and the citizen is the same as the one between the shopkeeper and the citizen or the one between the wage laborer and the citizen, and so on for many other distinctions in civil society.[13] To him, all these distinctions of a human being as a bourgeois have to disappear. He thinks that they will

13. Ibid., p. 9.

be of no importance in the future anyway, but before reaching that stage, we can actively do something to support the iron laws of historical development, namely try to delete all these distinctions and *make* them disappear.

Following that track of thinking, his writing suddenly becomes a very frightening piece, still forceful, but one that also causes a lot of trouble. Obviously, the essence of bourgeois society for Marx is egoism. In their bourgeois life people are egoistic, and what has to be done is to teach them to overcome their egoism and make them social: a question of social engineering, one could say, of designing the society. Marx says it explicitly: Man has to become a species being. There should no longer be egoistic individuals. So far, this goal has not been achieved: «Man was not freed from religion; he received religious freedom. He was not freed from property. He received freedom of property. He was not freed from the egoism of trade but received freedom to trade.»[14] And in the background of this we certainly hear the rhetorical bells ringing: let us finally free him from religion, let us finally free him from property, free him from all his egoism, let us finally make him a real species being! This species being is the true, the authentic human being.

And since we are in France, I would like to bring in another famous triad. It seems that the general subtext of his writing is a variation on the three famous words of the

---

14. Ibid., p. 20.

ON BRACKETS AND ON BEING A MARXIST-IN-A-CERTAIN-SENSE

French revolution: *liberté, egalité, fraternité*. About liberty and equality, Marx speaks quite a lot. But what do they mean? As *political* concept, liberty seems to mean nothing to him: it means that we are monads and do not relate to each other, it indicates something as an obstacle to real community. And the same goes for the political right of equality: Equality means that we all have the same right to be monads. Certainly, he also speaks about property, which is suspicious in the same sense. In *Capital* (vol. I, chapter 6) there is the famous saying: Liberty, Equality, Property and Bentham – that is the Garden of Eden. This is a nice, ironic, enumeration culminating in Bentham and his much-praised conviction that everybody's egoism will in the end be for the good of society and community.

So he speaks a lot about liberty and equality, but there is no mention of *fraternité*. Why doesn't he mention it? Well, maybe because the whole writing is exactly about this – without mentioning the word he speaks about the *idea of fraternité*. This is also the reason that the title of this writing – «On the Jewish Question» – which seems so arbitrary at first, is in fact very important. It plays exactly into the context that was mentioned at the beginning, in referring to your bracket and the triad of *communio, communism* and *communitarianism*. The fact that his approach could have something to do with what was traditionally religion, with what the Jewish religion was, that the aspect of communality plays an important role: this is completely left aside by Marx in his writing.

I don't know whether at the end I should really put this into a question. But there is something that I find very remarkable in this piece by Marx. It is something that he wrote, when he was only about 25 years old, and he is still much more philosophical than in his later writings. Reading *Capital*, the discussion is so much about cotton and linen and spindles, and everything is so much centered on economy. But here it is different. He is still quite Hegelian and he wants to keep this philosophical approach, an approach to totality, an approach to philosophy. Certainly, he wants to criticize it, he wants to turn things up and down, as his famous saying goes, but he wants to apply philosophy to society, he wants to do something with it for society, for our being together and living together. So my question is the following: How can we preserve and how can we take up this enormous potential of protest – and I think that you mentioned before that you appreciate exactly this potential – for a counter movement? It is remarkable that today we are discussing very similar questions in the context of communitarianism and a general protest against the egotistical society, questions that have already been touched upon by Marx. But how can we take up this protest, how can we make it a valuable ingredient of our considerations without falling into the abyss of social engineering or social designing? Thank you.

For Freedom, Against Emancipation.
Fraternity, Paternity, Sensibility
(Marx' Narrow Field of Vision)

JLN: No, thank *you*. You said you don't know how to put it into a question, but when you made it a question, there is no answer to it. How can we....?

You are totally right and I think you said something that is very important, something that has also been important for me over the last years and even before. But it is still underway. If we put the question as you did, namely how to use the enormous potential of protest without falling into what you called a designed society, it might be difficult. Maybe the strength of revolt has to come from somewhere else and in another way. Of course, Marx put his finger where it hurts and that, I think, is the question of the general equality and the becoming of a community. I think you are fully right: Precisely the fraternity, or what indicates fraternity, remains out of the field of vision. Maybe this is because, for Marx, it was something that would come about spontaneously, after the end of capitalism, the auto-transformation of capitalism would take place with just a little help from the revolution. But where, then, does the problem come from? For me, it comes precisely from the idea of emancipation. A few years ago, in an interview for a newspaper – I don't exactly remember the context – I said something that was not directed against emancipation but that tried to open the question of whether it is enough to speak of emancipation. And maybe some people were unhappy with it. But emancipation is a word that comes from Latin, it means the way of how a slave becomes free. And I would say that we are still in the same frame of the *polis* or the *civitas*, that is the place for the free people, and the free people are precisely those who are not slaves, neither slaves, nor women, nor children, nor strangers nor foreigners. At the beginning, the word emancipation has a clear meaning: namely to become a free man, to have all the rights related to being free in the *civitas*. But when it comes to modern society, where all the emancipation is done – and I think it is very interesting to take that text by Marx that you chose – then there is a difficulty: there is nothing more from which we would have to be emancipated. There is a freedom, namely the freedom of working. And the free work, as you know from Marx' *German Ideology*, is something like working in the morning, fishing in the afternoon, playing the cello in the evening. There is a sense of freedom in Marx, which would mean to open up for all the possibilities of being, of making and realizing sense. But he never really says how that would operate, e.g. playing the cello is very good, but what to play, why play? Alone? And whose work to play? Bach or Rimsky-Korsakov? There are a lot of questions that come *after* emancipation. And I think that all those questions are related to the idea of freedom. Marx still remains a modern man, a man of the freedom of the *libero arbitrio*. Curiously so many Marxists of my age in France have been Spinozists. But what does Spinoza say about freedom? He says that man is never free, only God is free. And I think that this passage in Spinoza is very important. It doesn't mean that God would be free only in the sense of making what he wants. No, as we know, God is a name for *natura naturans* or for substance, which means that the only freedom is the freedom of the all together, the freedom of everybody belonging to the whole, making sense only within the whole. This is related to something that Irina asked before. Communication has an influence, or think of what is called *l'effet papillon*, which means that what one does here has an effect everywhere. If, e.g. Bach writes a piece for cello, it has an effect not only on the musician of the time of Bach, but on the whole, and maybe even not only within the Western culture and the Western sensibility.

So, I agree fully with you, and I would say that this is a question for us, a question for tomorrow: What is freedom? And maybe even freedom is not the best name for it, but I don't know a better one. At least it is not only the freedom of being ‹free from…› (that is emancipation), but also the freedom of being ‹free *for*…› I would once again take up the example of the cello: in order to play the cello – to play any kind of music – it is necessary to practise every day, it is something which is absolutely not free. We know how Beethoven or Mozart were educated by their fathers – once again, we could say, a question of *paternité*. They were educated in a very strict, maybe even cold manner. But the exercise of music, the exercise of philosophy, the exercise of sport, the exercise of love, the exercise of being together need a lot of effort, something which is not exactly to be free.

Just one more word about fraternity. There is a place in Marx where he speaks about the workers at the end of the day drinking together in the pub and coming out to the street. And Marx says, when you see the faces of these brave people being so happy, maybe a little drunk, but not too much, then you get a sense of what humanity is. One could also call it a sense of human value. This relates back to the fact that Marx was all the time unable to say what value is – the pure value, which he very rarely speaks about, not the exchange value or the market value. There is the value of the man, the value of the worker who invests value into the thing that he is working on. Maybe his attention to the production and the process of working is the reason why his vision of value becomes too narrow.[15]

---

15. See Karl Marx, *Economic and Philosophic Manuscripts of 1844*, second Manuscript. First Published: Progress Publishers, Moscow 1959; Translated: by Martin Milligan from the German text, revised by Dirk J. Struik, contained in Marx/Engels, Gesamtausgabe, Abt. 1, Bd. 3. The passage reads: »When communist artisans associate with one another, theory, propaganda, etc., is their first end. But at the same time, as a result of this association, they acquire a new need – the need for society– and what appears as a means becomes an end. In this practical process the most splendid results are to be observed whenever French socialist workers are seen together. Such things as smoking, drinking, eating, etc., are no longer means of contact or means that bring them together. Company, association, and conversation, which again has society as its end,

And another thing I want to say about fraternity: the concept of fraternity has been a very strong point of the discussion between Derrida and myself as well as between myself and Blanchot, who were the people of fraternity *and* community. Derrida absolutely didn't like community, maybe because it was too close to the Jewish religious community. In that way he was closer to Marx. Also, fraternity for him was related to phallogocentrism, the father etc. I wanted to write and answer him but it was too late. But I wrote it anyway. So far, I guess, it is only published in Turkish, but later it will also come out in French. My only argument is that fraternity is precisely without the father. Fraternity starts when the father is dead. You can take Freud as a source here, from Freud to Lacan. So what does fraternity mean? It means to be together without a consistent cause for being together. Maybe this is my feeling of a family. I am from a family of five. And I always think that it is strange to be a family, because we do not have very much in common. Nobody feels the blood, or the origin etc. Of course, all the stories about family and fraternity, fraternity of blood, even fraternity of nation, are made by the desire to find a unity and an intimacy. But the truth of fraternity is precisely to be *without* any common thing.

If fraternity is the name for sensibility – I don't like the word, but I can't find a better one – if fraternity is the name

<blockquote>
are enough for them; the brotherhood of man is no mere phrase with them, but a fact of life, and the nobility of man shines upon us from their work-hardened bodies».
</blockquote>

for a common sensibility, then it means that it is the sensibility of the many, alone, together, having as the starting point nothing that tells them: you are the same family.

Alienation: «How Much Heimat does One Need?»

PARTICIPANT: Do you think that for Marx freedom is a freedom without alienation?

JLN: That freedom means to be without alienation? For a second I was thinking about that word in the context of emancipation. It is almost the same question in a more Hegelian way. Alienation or *Entfremdung* means being first not being at home, at the *Heimat* (you Irina spoke about *Heimat*). There is a chapter in a book by Jean Améry, who was a Belgian that survived the camp, with the title «How much *Heimat* do we need?»[16] In the camp there is absolutely no *Heimat*, and then you feel that you need a *Heimat*.

Alienation is Hegelian because it can be understood very clearly in the Hegelian way of first having the «in itself», secondly the «for itself» and thirdly the «in and for itself». So you can only start the process of *Entfremdung*, of becom-

16. Jean Améry. »Wieviel Heimat braucht der Mensch?«. In: *Jenseits von Schuld und Sühne. Bewältigungsversuche eines Überwältigten.* Stuttgart, Klett-Cotta, 1977, 2. Aufl. 1980.

ing alienated, foreign to the self, if you have a self. But also the first point, the «in itself», is totally abstract, says Hegel himself. The dialectical process of alienation is then a process of coming from abstraction to concretion, to the concrete totality, which is being, real being, precisely the first being. Being as the starting-point in science – as Hegel states at the beginning of the *Greater Logic*– is the purest and emptiest notion. When we take alienation apart from this Hegelian scheme, how could we then designate the first self, from which we would go out and to which implicitly we should come back? That is a point – similar to the question of emancipation – about which Marx says nothing. And the problem, maybe, is that we should think in another way than in that of the thinking of the self. The whole question is that of returning to the self as another in order to become the self. As Heidegger writes in the *Beiträge*, the self by itself is only a coming to the self, a return to it. The self is a return. The self is no thing, is not a one, but a process. It is a process of becoming, because there is no self. Consider the famous phrase «Become the one you are». It is not by chance that this is a very weak expression of the modern world. «Become the one you are» presupposes that the «one» is somewhere given. At the last moment, I can become the one I am. The one I am at the end is the one who is there. There is no return. For that reason, the concept of alienation is maybe *le maillon le plus faible*, as Lenin could have said, the weakest part in the chain of Marxist representation.

«Dass uns erst im Verlust des Verlorenen aufscheint, was uns gehört» or Presence vs. Tension (How to Think Sensibility and Desire?)

GUSTAV STRANDBERG: I would also like to address the problem of being-with, perhaps especially in relation to what we might call its fragile or broken nature. As Professor Nancy has emphasized, we are beings-with from the moment of our birth, from the moment of our entry into the world. This being-with – this being-in-common – is an in-common with the world as well as with other people at the same time. But this being-with is at the same time a being-in-common that is in a constant tension between the appearance and the disappearance of the common. Or, as you yourself have phrased it, there is a kind of interplay between the auto-destruction and the auto-construction of a sense of community. So this kind of in-between in tension or, as one might call it, the tense in-between, suggests that this between, the «with» of the being-with, manifests itself as concealing and appearing at the same time. The loss of the between, the loss of the common and the «loss of the common ground» (the title of our project) is then a constitutive part of the between itself. In fact, it is in and through the loss of the common that the common as such manifests itself. It is, as Heidegger once wrote in a quite beautiful passage in *Der Satz vom Grunde*, only in the loss of what has been lost that what belongs to us first appears, or in German, «dass uns erst im Verlust des Verlorenen aufscheint, was uns gehört»[17]. In other words, our being-with is therefore never a pure presence, which would be the dream of capitalism. It is a broken between which precisely through its broken finitude has the power to be this in-between, this *inter-esse* without being a particular interest. As you have written, presence in fact is only presence as co-presence. But this «co-» or «with» cannot in itself be brought to presence, but exists only as this tension, the poles of which pull us together and tear us apart as a community. They both appear and disappear at the same time, in a kind of an intertwined interaction. I am going to keep my question short, but this leads me to the question of how we are to understand this tension, and whether tension is a good conceptual term to describe this. How is this tension to be understood in relation to the appearance and disappearance of the community?

The other question that I have written down is not the one that I am going to ask you now, because it concerns the relation of being-with and the question of history. Your first reply to Irina was already quite informative concerning history. Instead I want to return to what you brought up under the heading of sensibility, but perhaps more towards the relation of sensibility, affection and desire. It is a question that, I know, you have asked before. How are we to understand the relation between sensibility and desire, if one has to admit that the individual, the subject, the Ego is not a legiti-

---

17. Heidegger. *Der Satz vom Grund,* (Stuttgart: Klett-Cotta, 2006), p. 101.

mate starting point for this question. This entails, in a sense, that the psychoanalytic tradition has started from the wrong foundation, which would be that of the individual. The criticism that is often directed against the phenomenological tradition, when it comes to questions of politics, concerns precisely this, namely that phenomenology, even in its doctrine of passive synthesis, is incapable of thinking desire, at least if what concerns us is an active form of desire that would constitute a rupture within reason itself. So my question is the following: How are we to think the relation between sensibility and desire, if it is neither through the psychoanalytic nor through the phenomenological tradition?

One that is Bigger than Subject: «Chaque fois unique, la fin du monde», or, God's Desire: «Cannot Not Do»

JLN:[18] Certainement, il faudrait revenir sur ces synthèses passives. Je ne suis pas compétent pour en parler à brûle-pourpoint. Je dirais seulement que même la passivité husserlienne reste celle d'un sujet. Je m'intéresse plus à une passivité plus

18. Certainly, it would be necessary to go back to these passive syntheses. I am not competent to speak about these at point-blank range, as it were. I would just say that even passivity, in a Husserlian sense, remains that of a subject. I am more interested in a more radical passivity – or more properly one without roots – and in a ‹being-affected› which precedes any kind of being.

radicale – ou plutôt sans racines – et à un être-affecté qui précède toute espèce d' «être»...

One should, though, make a distinction between fragile and broken, for they are not the same. Broken follows from a solidity-unity, fragility is a permanent state of in-jeopardy-of-being-broken. But that means here: there is no solidity, no given unity; there is the relation as such, which exists only as «fragile», that is never taken as given and granted.

I agree with the term «tension» and with understanding the word «tension» itself as desire – desire meant in a non-psychoanalytic way. With Lacan, in fact, this is very complicated, as are many other things in Lacan. The question of desire is most clearly exposed by Freud, when he asks in relation to sexual desire how it is possible that the intention of a process can produce a pleasure that is what he calls a preliminary pleasure. Because for him, the real or true pleasure is final pleasure. But then final pleasure would mean the end of tension. This is something like entropy. And, just to stay with Freud, it is a paradox that what goes beyond the pleasure principle, namely the death drive, is in fact – as Derrida shows very clearly and rightly in *Spéculer – sur «Freud»* [19] – still submitted to the pleasure principle. This is so because death is the pleasure of entropy. So there is, as Derrida says, no beyond the principle of pleasure. But if there is no such

---

19. Jacques Derrida, «Spéculer sur «Freud»» in: *La carte postale de Socrate à Freud et au-delà*, Paris: Aubier-Flammarion 1980.

beyond the pleasure principle, this also means that there is no entropy. Entropy itself shall be in a tension in itself or toward itself. Once again it is the «itself»...

I am coming back to the beginning of your question now. You claimed that there is a tension between appearance and disappearance of the common. When you were born, it was not your appearance, but it was the appearance of the common for the little, little small subject – not a «little subject» only because you were a baby or because even now as a big man you are still very small. But much more in the sense of Freud: that the Ego constitutes only the very small surface of the big mass of the Id. But the Id is so much of you and so real that it is the whole not only of you but of the whole of the world. In the Id there are animals, plants, even minerals, all that is in this very small point, Freud says: *le disque germinatif*, which I am, where I am supposed to be. But precisely to be here is only to present a point at one place on the surface of the Id or of the world in general. I like to say that the unconscious is the world, it is not something inside of the world – it *is* the world.

On one level, I would like to try to think without subjectivity as far as it is possible, or more precisely: to think a subjectivity without a «sub-jectum»; but in the infinite tension and opening out which is the «being» of «one» who as such is no-thing. But I know this is not possible in an absolute way. Or maybe it is possible to think about a subject without subjectivity – or a «one» without «interiority». But this is not the topic now. And so we can return to your formula of «between appearance and disappearance of the common». It is true: for a subject, for each one, there is appearance and disappearance of the being in common, but this appearance and disappearance is at the same time the appearance and disappearance of me. Before I was born, I was not here, and after my death I will no longer be here. I know this is very fragile. It is complicated to try to speak beyond subjectivity, but still to pay attention to the oneness, which is maybe less than subjectivity, less or maybe more than subjectivity. At least it is not necessary to think that in the religions – religions as they were, before God left the earth – or in art and literature, we are not in the condition of this very small «one». Maybe we can touch upon that with the question, the well-known question: What is an artist? or Who is an artist? We know very well today that the artist is not Leonardo da Vinci. But nevertheless it is not nobody. Somewhere, there is Leonardo. And somewhere Leonardo is something like the point of speaking about the genius. What is a genius? Today we are not allowed to use this cliché. But in that case, let's ask: What was once understood under the name genius or – if you want – under the name of the Muses? Oneness. I was friend with a painter, the well-known painter Simon Hantaï. He was French, but came from Hungary. And he liked to say: ‹I am not the author, I am not the painter, I do nothing but being on the floor.› He had invented a way of folding and unfolding paper. And once he said: ‹It's just mechanical work. Everybody can do that.› I said: ‹But I can't.› And then he answered: ‹No, you cannot.› ‹Why?› ‹Because only I can do that, but it's not me.› This is exactly the point: «only you» (as the song goes) – but you are not you! The tension then is maybe the tension between me and me, it is in-between the one who I am, the one who in truth appears and disappears and with whom the whole world appears and disappears. I am thinking now of the phrase of Derrida which he used for the title of the book in which somebody collected all his eulogies and funeral speeches. The title is *Chaque fois unique, la fin du monde*[20] – each time the end of the world, of *the* world. And I remember that afterwards in many French newspapers they wrote about the book saying ‹each time the end of one world›. He became very angry with them and said: ‹They don't understand the point, the point is that each time is the end of *the* world.› This really opens another dimension: How to think the world as all the time being a process of appearing and disappearing? Maybe this is precisely what we have to think about. The world is not a continuity of... well, a continuity of what? A continuity of time. But not because time is entirely in the world. As Kant says, everything is in time, except for time itself. Where is time itself? Time itself is time. I would say that it is not about continuity but the opening of the reason for appearance and disappearance. Of course, the time of Kant is exactly not this one. Because there

---

20. Jacques Derrida. *Chaque fois unique, la fin du monde* (Paris: Editions Galilée, 2003)

is nothing new and nothing comes to the end in time for Kant. But this, I would say, is already a modern and chronometrical understanding of time. It is the time, which Kant would represent by a line. But time as reason is something else. Time as reason starts with the day, it starts with day and night, every day. The whole cosmos is made of it.

Then we can maybe return to tension as the rule of reason. Just a last word to come back to the *inter* or *between*. Reason is made, exactly, out of the between. There is no reason, if there is no between. And maybe with reason it is the same as with the one and time in the beginning. There is reason because there is a between. The between is the way in which each time is in relation to and in tension with another.

Just one more thing concerning the concept of desire – there is a strange thing in all the classical descriptions of the creation of the world. One could put it very simply, referring to Descartes, Leibniz, Malebranche (not to Spinoza, because there is no creation in Spinoza). In all of them there is a tension precisely between inside God who has to create the world and cannot not do that. God «cannot not,» not because He would be forced to do that but because «God» is nothing else than the existence of the world. So, then, there is a necessity in God. Or there is no necessity in God and he is free to create the world. But why do it? Because of a kind of desire! Then we would come to the question, if it is a good or a bad desire and so on. But we leave that.

Myth with Plato, Mythos with Platonov, or, is Literature Sacrifice?

MCS: Keeping the thread of the loss of the subject or of subjectivity as connected to sensibility and desire, maybe it would be possible to ask why the discourse, or should we say the «myth» of the subject, of the self is so powerful? Or should we first ask about myth as such?

TORA LANE: I would like to take the opportunity now and ask you about the relation between literature, community and myth. I am thinking more specifically about the way you address this question in *The Inoperative Community* and *Myth Interrupted*. Coming from Russian studies and doing my research on the work of the Soviet writer Andrei Platonov (1899-1952), I saw a very stimulating tension between his ideas and your own concerning this relation. I see a question that both of you pose in your works, namely, the question about what writing can be in the modern condition of the «absence of», of «without» grounds. You speak about writing in the condition of an absence of «myth»; Platonov asks this question in relation to what he calls absence of truth and sense. What is the difference? Is there a difference? We are now more and more used to speaking about the myth of truth and sense but even of the truth and sense of myth. But how to think these questions when you define literature: as the trajectory of sense that absents itself? You wrote once that:

Literature traces the infinite journey of sense in so far as it absents itself. This self-absenting of sense is not negative, it is sense's chance and what is at stake in it as such. To ‹write› means relentlessly to approach the limit of speech, that limit which speech alone touches and in touching it un-limits us (we speaking beings), de-subjectivizes us.[21]

Perhaps the limits of speech are also what points toward its groundlessness, its senselessness, and precisely the recognition of this is at the same time a recognition of how sense is present and absent, is both caught and evades, and therefore what i-(un-)limits us? Do you think this trajectory of sense that absents itself should be understood as sacrifice, as Blanchot proposed, when he talked about «the sign of great realities that one attains by means of a tragic effort against oneself»?[22] Is this sacrifice, let us say the «mythical sacrifice», the sacrifice of the subject and a certain relation to an intelligible and readable world, the sacrifice of intelligibility? These reflections make me think about the Russian poet Marina Tsvetaeva who thinks sacrifice as the sacrifice of the historical subject, and the beginning of the literary subject, and again of Platonov who speaks about the sacrifice of the ‹bourgeois› I, and the beginning of the no-

21. Jean-Luc Nancy »Maurice Blanchot, 1907-2003» in *Paragraph* nr. 30, p. 3 2007.
22. Maurice Blanchot, *Faux Pas*, Paris:Gallimard, 1943, p. 222.

body – the nameless, the fatherless, with no clear goal for the journey and nothing to lose. In the way that Platonov's most deprived, and therefore most exposed heroes fail in their relation to the world, another world of senseless sense begins to emerge. At the end of his novel *Happy Moscow*,[23] the hero, following the sacrifice of his name and his status, enters the home of a poor woman and takes the place of her late husband. This family is full of contempt towards him, yet now he can feel happiness. In the novel, the word happiness acquires existential meaning only here, in the most unhappy and meaningless of existences. In the sacrifice of all supposed meaning, the word acquires meaning. Is there a relation between the loss of myth, the sacrifice of intelligibility and the appearance of the limits of sense?

JLN: First I have to say that I don't know Platonov. It's shameful to say that, but I have never read a book of Platonov. I know I have to, but, well... Maybe if I would, I would be better able to answer your question. But if I understood correctly what was said at the beginning, your question could be simply: is the absence of myth the same as the absence of truth and sense? Absence of myth being the one of Jean-Luc Nancy and absence of truth and sense the one of Platonov?

23. Andrey Platonov. *Happy Moscow*, trans. Robert and Elizabeth Chandler with Angela Livingstone, Nadya Bourova, and Eric Naiman (London: Hardville Press, 1999)

TL: Would it then also be possible to say that the absence of myth is the beginning of the absence of truth and sense?

JLN: This is always the main difficulty with myth – that is, how the word is understood. If myth in Platonov is understood, as you said, as the end of truth, then we come back to Plato, and myth becomes a name for fiction, and fiction for not being true. But we know that this word myth, that is the Greek word *mythos*, was taken by Plato for the first time more or less, that is, in this critical meaning. But, as you know, for Homer, for Hesiod, *mythos* does absolutely not have this meaning, because Homer and Hesiod are only writing what we call *mythos*. In the Greek of Homer, *mythos* is, if I remember correctly, the word as it is said and *epos* is the word as an entirety of something that is said. *Mythos, mythoi*; there is in Homer a passage in which the Greek word *mythos* is connected with wings – he speaks about winged words[24]. The wing is the image for the word coming out of the mouth and flying. Thus the designation of myth, that is, of a story which is a fiction, is then a story that nobody will consider as a true story. That is the status of the story in Homer or the story or cosmogony of Hesiod. No one reading or listening to Homer's songs – because they *were* songs – believed that they were the truth, as we understand it. But everybody did know through what

---

24. Homer's expression is ἔπεα πτερόεντα – épea pteróenta, it appears 46 times in the Iliad and 58 times in the Odyssey.

meaning they should be known; everybody did know that it was the story of the Greeks, the story of the war between the Greeks, or all the Greeks together, against the Trojans etc., and then the story of Ulysses' return home etc. Maybe we are no longer able to grasp this way of taking the story as a story, something that is both more and less than an understanding, something which has in itself something to which I am related in one way or another, that is, in the final instance, myth. So, this kind of story – a story, as is often said, about origin, about the beginning, the foundation – that is, a story about the ground, a story which tells the story departing from the very beginning, as theogony, that is, as the birth of the gods. One cannot go a step before that. I would say that the status of the listener of Homer or Hesiod is not the same status as the one who has to understand, to appreciate and to determine if it is true or not. Nobody is there to say «no, it didn't happen in that way; no, Agamemnon did not do that with Iphigenia» etc. I would say, then, that what Plato named as myth and in the meaning that it still has for us (and I think the same is operating in Platonov, based on what you have said), that opposes myth to truth, should rather be grasped from the difference between false and true *mythos*, the true speaking, the true logos. True mythos is logos, logos as logos, which comes to be opposed to *mythos*, because logos has one main claim, in a certain way, it has only one claim, that is, to bring with itself, with logos, the way to demonstrate that it is coherent with itself. That is, logos is the speech, if you want, or the word that is able to found itself, to be its own foundation, and the main thing with myth, that is, myth in the sense of Homer and Hesiod, and in the sense of everything we call myth in all mythical cultures, the main thing is that myth does not try to demonstrate its own ability to found itself. It tells something. I tell you the story, and the story (and I think that we could say this of every literary story as well) is or has its own value in itself, as a story. Nobody is there to say «no, that is not true, that can't be, it cannot have happened in that way» etc. But for me, in my own terms, this is precisely what I would call *sense*. So I would not take truth and sense together. In the book *The Sense of the World*[25], I wrote that the truth is an interruption of sense. Truth, then, is neither verification nor sense. Truth is what has no ground, no foundation. Maybe it comes back to the relation between appearance and disappearance, maybe truth is appearance and disappearance, the in-between, and the tension is sense, but this tension is precisely and exactly the tension of the narrative.

What is a narrative? Narrative does not mean only that one thing is said, and then afterward another thing; above all, it also does not mean that there is an *intrigue, comment dire*, a plot. The question is not about beginning, about the time of narrative, plot etc. The main thing is, I would say, that the story has no beginning and no end, or better,

---

25. Jean-Luc Nancy. *The Sense of the World* (Minneapolis: The University of Minnesota Press, 1997)

that it starts before its own beginning and goes beyond its own end. Take a novel by Platonov. As in any novel, when it starts, you understand at least two things: there is something that starts, it is the first day of something, but something already started before. Take the beginning of the Iliad: «*Mēnin aeide: thea Pēlēiadeō Akhilēos oulomenen...*»[26] You see, there is a piece of advice there, but we will leave the *thea*, the goddess there on the side of the genius. Think, the *colère*, the anger of Achilles, so Achilles is angry or was angry, so it has already happened, and at the end you can look at the last line of the Iliad: it is not finished, there is something more. There are some beginnings and some ends, some novels are more remarkable than others, but, and you know that there is the typical beginning of the tale – one day, or once upon a time. A time, it was a time, so there was another time before, but at this time, precisely, upon a time, I don't know, once upon a time, Bluebeard enters the castle, etc. and *there*, there is something which is very close to music, that is then not too much a logic, but is close to music in that when the music starts it has already started. The first sound of a piece of music is the first, but you can hear it only by hearing at the same time something, the pre-sound of

---

26. »Homère, *Iliade*, vers 1-2 (Paris: Les Belles Lettres, 1972), p. 2 »Chante, déesse, le colère d'Achille, le fils de Pélée; détestable colère...» English Version »Achilles' wrath, to Greece the direful spring/of woes unnumber'd, heavenly goddess, sing!» In *Homer*, trans. Alexander Pope (London: Penguin Books, 1996), p. 50

the sound itself. And, as you know, at the end of the sound – when does the sound end? At the end of a concert, it is very interesting to see how long the people wait before they start to applaud. They wait, and it is not out of respect, or of a kind of religiosity, but people are listening to the rest, and the infinite rest of the song. In a way, some people feel that it would be better not to make any noise, not to applaud. It is not easy not to make any noise, because everybody would feel an enormous void, an infinity. But this is the truth, that is the truth as a void.

Now, I am looking at the last note I wrote as you were speaking: «literature as the sacrifice of intelligibility» – I would say yes. Yes, [a sacrifice] of the intelligibility of a beginning and an end, of a foundation and an achievement, but this intelligibility is precisely only the intelligibility of the one who expects the possibility of, I think – and I can find no other word – of a verification. Verification means to make truth, *veri facere* – literature, precisely – and then the mythical nature of literature as sacrifice, *sacrum facere*, is the sacrifice of the very «fice», if I can say that. But the sacrifice of the truth, in that sense, is the understanding that what is at stake is not precisely verification, but is, and maybe I think of the word Bailly used as a title for a small book about Lacoue-Labarthe – the *veridiction*[27]. That is, to tell the truth does not have the

---

27. Jean-Christophe Bailly. *La veridiction: sur Lacoue-Labarthe*, (Paris: Bourgeois, 2011)

meaning of verification, of telling the truth to the police – where you were, what you did – so that the police can verify if it is true. Veridiction is a word that means the proper gesture of the writer, when it is precisely another truth, that is, the truth which is precisely the truth which shows itself as truth by showing that it was already there before, and will be there after. Now, lastly, we could say ok, but why is literature for us, and certainly (I guess) for Platonov, or rather: why does literature not have the strength of...the common strength of the myth – that is, of the foundation of a community? I have no answer, because, one could say, of course, this is because literature is no longer in the realm of religion. Literature does not tell a story of gods, that is, of real foundation, but after Homer literature, *epos,* wants to narrate a foundation; the first testimony of this, I think, is the *Aeneid* of Virgil. Virgil writes the *Aeneid* in order to narrate, or, he makes the narrative of the foundation of Rome. But, and there are wonderful pages in the *Aeneid*, the *Aeneid* has the small defect of being a piece of the Empire and the Emperor, and so shows that it is presenting this foundation. Considering then – and there are poorer *epoi* like *The Henriade* of Voltaire for example – Cervantes, Balzac, Proust, Tolstoy and Platonov maybe, Faulkner, don't we have there a myth of our world? Myth in the sense of Homer. My feeling would be (and I cannot say that this is a thought) that yes, we have our mythology, but we are not able to take it or to grasp it as such. Nevertheless, we do it, because we read books, and because a new writer starts to write new books, and of course it is clear that the use of the myth and particularly of the Aryan myth, etc. in Nazism is absolutely something that did not happen by chance...

MCS: Maybe at this point we could try to approach the same question about the being-without, that is, being with myth without being able to take it or grasp it as such, and try to formulate the question of how this being-with and being-without are and are not the same?

L'être sans comme fond sans fond de l'être avec (Being-Without as the Ground Without Ground of Being-With)

VICTORIA FARELD:[28] Je voudrais suivre cette insistance autour de la question d'être avec, *Mitsein*, being-with; plus précisément autour du rapport entre être avec et être sans, dans quelle mesure cette expérience d'être avec pourrait se décrire comme un mode de vivre la condition d'être fondamentalement sans: *Ohnesein*, being-without; et dans l'extension de cette réflexion comment articuler l'être avec, comme, justement, une expérience d'être sans au cœur d'une ontologie corporelle?

Pour tout d'abord vous donner le contexte de ma ques-

---

28. English translation on page 103 ff.

tion: Dans mon travail de doctorat, je me suis intéressé par la question de la reconnaissance – *Anerkennung*/Recognition. Ce qui m'a intéressé était une certaine schizophrénie au cœur du débat de la politique de la reconnaissance: même si la discussion du désir de la reconnaissance tournait autour de la dépendance constitutive des autres au fond de notre existence, elle a tout de même reproduit un idéal de l'autonomie et de l'indépendance, à travers la communauté.

La reconnaissance est, autrement dit, traitée uniquement comme une force appropriatrice avec laquelle on gagne accès à soi-même à travers les autres, et non pas comme une force expropriatrice qui signale plutôt une perte, une perte constitutive originaire, du rapport entre, justement, le soi et la possession. Dans ce travail, j'ai essayé de trouver une autre façon de parler de la reconnaissance, qui prend sa force expropriatrice du propre comme point de départ.

Bon. Dans mon travail actuel, j'ai voulu continuer à explorer les ressources philosophiques pour thématiser l'expérience de l'exposition, de l'expropriation, de la dépendance fondamentale, de la vulnérabilité, au fond de notre existence, notre coexistence. Même si j'ai lâché la question de reconnaissance, je suis quand même, on pourrait dire, restée en moitié dans ce mot; je suis restée dans la deuxième partie du mot: naissance.

Une expérience très, peut-être même trop, concrète de «venir à la coexistence – ‹of coming into being or into coexistence› – est la naissance». C'est très symptomatique que l'histoire de la philosophie a montré très peu d'intérêt, finalement, aux expériences liées à la naissance, et à l'enfance (avec quelques exceptions importantes bien-sûr). Ce qui donne le ton est plutôt l'idée que ces expériences de dépendance, d'exposition et de vulnérabilité, liées à la naissance et l'enfance montrent que des stades à dépasser.

Descartes dans son *Discours de la méthode* regrette que l'homme ne soit pas né adulte. L'enfance représente un état de manque ou d'insuffisance. Devenir adulte est une déclaration d'indépendance (à la Kant): *Selbstständigkeit*, dans le sens original du mot – *selber, aus eigener Kraft stehen können*.

Cette ‹adultocentrisme› si présente dans l'historie de la philosophie signale, je trouve, une résistance à vouloir accepter l'exposition même qui donne le rapport, la coexistence, l'exposition qui nous rend possible. Nous sommes, et non seulement à la naissance ou à l'enfance, nous restons, fondamentalement dépendent de ce qui est hors de nous pour que nos vies soient vivables; nos corps sont exposés de blessures, de maladies, du froid, de la chaleur, de la faim, de la soif, d'amour, du désir.

Dans votre pensée, j'ai trouvé une langue dans la langue pour exprimer les idées constitutives d'être avec en étant, justement, sans. L'être avec signale un mode d'être en commun sans être commun, une communauté sans totalité. Comme vous écrivez dans *L'expérience de la liberté*: «sans aucun rapport, et par cela même jetées dans le rapport»[29], nous parta-

---

29. Jean-Luc Nancy. *L'expérience de la liberté* (Paris: Galilée, 1988), p. 93.

geons quelque chose que nous n'avons pas; exprimé par vous de façon poétique: «nous est partagé cela qui nous partage» [*uns ist geteilt, das was uns teilt*][30].

Alors, au fond de notre coexistence, notre *Mitsein*, il y a *Ohnesein* dans le sens d'être sans, mais aussi dans le sens «sans être»; dans le sens du retrait de l'être pour le rapport; de l'être qui se retire en donnant le rapport: l'être avec, Mitsein; ou bien l'entre-être.

L'avec alors expose en effet le sans- le sans-commun. L'amour, l'acte sexuel, l'orgasme expriment cette impossibilité d'être en commun. Mais, l'événement qui marque, peut-être avec la plus de violence, cette impossibilité est, je voudrais dire, la naissance. La naissance est un moment qui permet d'expériencer la coexistantialité, l'être avec, comme, justement, un mode d'être sans.

Les deux corps qui se séparent et qui, dans le moment de séparation même, qui est le moment de la naissance, entrent dans le rapport; dans l'entre-être en fait. Je pense que la naissance comme question philosophique nous permettrait, donc, de penser l'être sans [très proche à l'être sens – avec un -e] comme fond sans fond de l'être avec si vous voulez, en affirmant l'extériorité des corps – très important – des corps finis et pluriels.

C'est important, je trouve, d'essayer de trouver une langue dans la langue, une position, qui permet d'expri-

---

30. ibidem, p. 95

mer/ de penser la corporalité [la corporealité peut-être] de l'entre-être.

En même temps, j'hesite. Ça serait quoi? Une ontologie corporelle de la coexistence qui a comme point de départ l'exposition, la vulnérabilité, la dépendance et qui nous permettrait d'articuler l'expérience d'être sans au cœur de la coexistence; une ontologie qui en même temps par nécessité serait une ontologie sociale et politique (être corps est être exposé aussi par des forces sociales et politiques; en étant un corps ‹humain› on ne peut pas exister hors de son organisation sociale et politique).

Ce que j'aimerais discuter avec vous c'est premièrement l'idée même de vouloir mettre non pas la raison, non pas la socialité ou la finitude de l'homme, mais la dépendance absolue de l'entre-être, comme point de départ pour une réflexion philosophique, disons «politique»; quel serait l'appel éthique d'un tel projet [s'il y en a] ?

Et quels seraient les dangers– en sachant que vulnérabilité, fragilité, exposition sont devenus des mots de clé dans un vocabulaire politique contemporain de la société de prévention, de l'industrie de sécurité ou nous sommes présentés comme exposés l'un de l'autre, exposés des menaces qui viennent hors de nous. Mais aussi au niveau plus philosophique: qu'est-ce ça veut dire de mettre cette idée d'être sans au cœur de l'être avec comme fondement d'une réflexion, d'une ontologie, finalement?

JLN:[31] Je suis entièrement d'accord. Je dois seulement vous rappeler que Hannah Arendt accorde, elle, un privilège à la naissance, à la «natalité». En français ce mot désigne plutôt un taux de naissance dans une population, comme «mortalité» d'ailleurs mais ce dernier mot peut aussi être compris comme «caractère d'être mortel». Et Arendt veut parler d'un caractère d'être «naissant», «natal», «à naître» comme vous voudrez. Pour elle c'est la vertu propre du commencement, de l'innovation. Je ne vais pas m'attarder sur elle, il nous faudrait les textes. Je souligne plutôt ceci: Arendt a certainement pensé cette natalité en contrepoint de «*Sein zum Tode*» de Heidegger. L'être – ou l'étant – qui naît est aussi seul à naître qu'il le sera à mourir. Aussi seul et aussi «avec» (car je pense que la mort est aussi «avec», malgré tout). Principiellement «avec» même et c'est ce que vous dites: naître, se séparer, s'individuer, entrer dans la relation. Et comme dit Freud, nous naissons toute notre vie. Tout le temps nous recommençons la relation, des relations, des rapports, des envois, des renvois, nous recevons et nous adressons...

Pour ma part je n'insisterais pourtant pas sur la vulnérabilité et la dépendance: ce sont des façons de dire qui sont adossées plus ou moins consciemment à l'image d'un individu autonome, complet, autosuffisant, comme si c'était là ce qui au fond devrait être. Et c'est au nom de cela qu'aujourd'hui se répand le schéma du «care», du soin et

---

31. English translation on page 107 ff.

du prendre soin... Certes il faut prendre soin lorsque c'est nécessaire. Mais le vrai soin n'est-il pas de remettre l'autre à sa (re)naissance? (En fait en disant cela je paraphrase un passage de Heidegger sur la «*Fürsorge*».). N'est-il-pas un «Vas-y! recommence!»? Par exemple un bon médecin est celui qui sait «lâcher» le malade pour le laisser retourner à la vie ordinaire avec ses risques, ses incertitudes et même la possibilité que la maladie y reprenne un élan... Si le soin envahit la vie, il ne soigne plus. Au contraire il faut que le soin sache se renoncer.

«Exposition» n'est pas «vulnérabilité», c'est ex-ister, ek-sister. Comme vous dites, nous sommes dans une société de sécurité maximale... et nous comprenons que cela même est un danger! L'exposition, c'est l'exposition au «sans» qui est au cœur du «avec»...

Second Day: At Nancy's home

It is another day. The sunlight is brighter, the trees are rose coloured and in blossom. We took the tramway to come to Jean-Luc Nancy's home. In comparing Sweden and northern France, one remarks upon the delay of the coming of spring in the Nordic countries. We arrived to a very welcoming home, to the hestia of the philosopher, to his books, paintings, and warmth. From his window, we could see the cathedral of Strasbourg, the highest in Europe, built of bricks, grès rose des Vosges, ressemblant des églises de sable *(the rose-colored stone of the Vosges, resembling sand-churches). We haven't planned the discussion today, but the question of arriving with a without remained.*

MCS:[32] Pour arriver à Strasbourg on a fait un petit détour par la tour de Hölderlin. Nous sommes arrivez à Karlsruhe et avons décidé de commencer notre voyage vers vous en passant par Hölderlin, par la solitude de Hölderlin, en començant ce voyage-promenade par le sol de la poésie. Hölderlin a écrit un poème appélé *Der Spaziergang*, Promenade, où se trouvent les vers:

---

32. English translation on page 109.

Ihr lieblichen Bilder im Tale,
Zum Beispiel Garten und Baum,
Und dann der Steg, der schmale,
Der Bach zu sehen kaum[33]

Ô jolies images du val,
Arbres et jardins, par exemple,
Et puis ce sentier très étroit,
Le ruisseau qu'on devine à peine[34]

You graceful views in the valley,
For instance garden and tree
And then the footbridge, the narrow,
The stream one can hardly see[35]

Ces images, les arbres et les jardins, «par exemple», «zum Beispiel», c'est à dire qui jouent en proximité...On passe par tant des images, dans la rue, dans les livres, dans la pensée, et puis on voit l'ètroit sentier, le ruisseau à deviner à peine... – je prend ces vers comme une epigraphe pour notre voyage-promenade vers vous, car le sens du sans qui nous hante reste étroit, à peine à deviner, parmi tant des images. (Je continue

33. Friedrih Hölderlin. »Der Spaziergang» in *Sämtliche* Werke, Beissner edition (Stuttgart: J. G. Cottasche/Kohlhammer, 1951), p. 276.
34. Hölderlin, »Promenade», trad. Gustav Roud, *Oeuvres*, ed. La Pléiade, (Paris: Gallimard, 1967), p. 1026.
35. Hölderlin, *The Walk,* trans. M. Hamburger in *Friedrich Hölderlin, Poems and Fragments* (London: Anvil Press, 2005), p. 755

en anglais, c'est plus facile, je pense pour tout le groupe). The sense of the without (*le sens du sans*) remains narrow, restricted, or perhaps we should say that it has to do with the narrowness and restraining character of a remainder.

Yesterday, before leaving the building of the University, I asked Jacob R. for his thoughts about the seminar and he said: «I think some students felt misled because they were expecting to hear, not so much a sociological discussion, as an ontological one...»

JLN: Sociological? I don't see where the sociology was...

MCS: Maybe there is a difficulty when the ontological discovers its own limits, or when the question is about the loss of the meaning of ontology discovering itself as the meaning of ontology, when the «without meaning» appears as the «meaning of the without», the without grounds as «ground» for «being-with». Should we put it in this way? This is a kind of *cercle carré* [squared circle], we can move without ends from with to without and the other way around. Should we today continue to move in this *cercle carré*, in this strange tautology of the «sens du sans» and the «sens sans»?

Trying to put together what was said yesterday and that was more clearly related to the question about the sense of the without, some phrases lingered in my mind. In discussing the meaning of the Greek *polis*, you insisted upon its novelty in inaugurating a being together without any given ground. The same motive or «image of thought», so to speak, appeared when you discussed the concept of «fraternity» as a being together without a consistent cause for being together, a fraternity that indeed is only really possible without the «father». We had a discussion about the self without a self, about sensibility and desire without the pressuposition of a self. It was said that in the loss of what is lost, what belongs to us may appear, and that in the absence of relations the being in relation appears as such. The common, the being-with, you said, is a mode of description of being without, that maybe could be understood as the «tension» between appearing and disappearing. We also talked about the sacrifice of intelligibility, about writing without reasons and implicitly about writing about the without reasons, about truth as «interruption of sense» and how the absence of myth meets the absence of truth and sense. Moreover, the question emerged of how to use the potential of protest without falling into a «designed society» and how this involves, we could say, the same question – how to protest without transforming protest into a new line of power, that is, into non-protest. At stake was the question about the threat of the appropriation of a discourse on being-with by techno-bureaucracy, the enhancement of power through an absorption of the critique of power by the institutions of power; the threat of the appropriation of critique by non-critique. Maybe we can say that these remains from yesterday show the «lines of senses», to use an expression of yours, the lines of sense of the «without»: If the being-with is without ground, does it mean that the «without ground» is the ground of the being-with? What is «ground» in this without ground? Should we begin with the sense of the «without»? What remained from the seminar yesterday resonates with several thoughts of yours in different books, and made me ask myself a question about our own research project – about «the loss of grounds as common ground»: what happens with the meaning of ground if it is to be thought from out of the narrowness and strictness of the «without»?

You said yesterday that you would like to hear from a very good specialist in English philology about the origin of the word ‹without›. I am not a very good specialist in English philology, but the etymology is I think ‹wiðutan›…, with the Scandinavian, Icelandic ‹ð›. And ‹wið› is the preposition ‹next to›…, by the side, *auprès de…*

JLN: The same as *apud* and *avec*

MCS: Precisely, but the Scandinavian ‹utan› is also ‹ohne› and ‹out›. It says something like *auprès de l'*outside, *auprès* de l'out. It seems that the expression «without» came into use around the 12th century, there might be an interesting sociological question about how it came into use, and so on… So, the point that was gathering in such different questions or comments yesterday is the idea that loss of a common ground as ground for the common should be understood as une *suspension du sens qui ouvre le ou plutôt du sens*[36]. Should we say, «without the ground» as both the meaning of ground and the grounding of meaning? I have in mind one fundamental passage of *La pensée finie* that I keep thinking and meditating about. You wrote: «L'absence du fondement (Abgründlichkeit) est ce qu'ici on transcrit par «le sens». L'absence du fondement n'est pas un manque de l'être à être soutenu, justifié, originé en tant qu'il est et en ce qu'il est. Elle est: que l'être ne renvoie à rien, ni à susbtance, ni à sujet, ni même à «être», sinon ou à d'un être-à, à soi, au monde, qui fait aussi bien l'ouverture, ou le je, l'être-jeté de l'existence»[37].

So, let's go back to the question of ground – not exactly back because we haven't been there yet, or perhaps we always have been there. Yesterday in answering Irina's question and comments, you said that «the *polis* is the name of the first togetherness in which no common ground of being together is given». When Plato proposed the *demiourgós* in the *Timaeus*, he says that «what appears has to have a cause». He understands «what appears» as something that

---

36. suspension of meaning as opening of meaning
37. Jean-Luc Nancy, *Une pensée finie*, (Paris: ed. Galilée, 1991), p. 19. «Here I transcribe groundlessness (*Abgründlichkeit*) as «sense». Groundlessness isn't a lack on the part of being that needs to be undergone, justified, originated. Rather, it is being's reference to nothing, either to substance or to subject, not even to «being», unless it be *to* being-to, to itself, to the world as the openness, the being-thrown of *existence*» in Jean-Luc Nancy. *A Finite Thinking*. (Stanford: Stanford University Press, 2003), p. 9.

was made, and as what exists insofar as a relation to what is being given is already estabished. He presents then the thesis that being is necessarily a *demiurgie, an oeuvre demiurgique*[38]. The problem involved in the affirmation that «what appears has to have a cause» could be rephrased in terms of *comment faire-apparaître le monde apparaisant?*[39] Then the answer is that it always appears out of a background. In your own terms: the image can only appear from a «fond de l'image», from the ground of the image. You made it possible, I think, to take another direction in relation to the question of ground when it is understood as «fond», as the «fond» of a canvas, for the question is how to *faire apparaître l'être apparaissant des choses*[40]. But when Plato proposes that what appears always appears in relation to something else (the cause), he says that it appears always together with this «other», together with the cause. That is why he not only speaks about *aitia*, but he uses the word *synaitia*, co-causes, conjoint or gathering causes[41]. He says that causality is a being-with. I think that this conjoinedness, this «co» implied in the concept of cause and ground, is a very central point in what we could call the demiurgical problem of the ground, as a ground for Western thought, because the Demiurge is the one who puts together the multiple and the

---

38. a demiurgic work
39. how to make appear the appearing of the world?
40. How to make appear the appearing being of things
41. See for example, *Timaeus*, 46d

diverse into a system of order, in the order of orders, into a coherent point. That is why I was wondering why you insist on the idea of *with-ness*, of «co-ness» when you think of *l'absence-de-fondement comme «le sens»* [the abence of ground as «the meaning»] ? Est-ce *qu'il n'a* pas *un certain platonisme* dans une pensée de l'être comme l'être-avec? *Est-ce que l'être-avec* ne garde toujours la promesse *d'une causalité qui à la fin* obstaculerait l'ouverture *pour une penseé de l'existence sans raison d'être?*[42] Why not ‹entre-être›, in-between being, compris comme en-train-d'être, dans le sens plus gérondif, an expression that you also used a few times? Or would it be a difference between a gerundive and a transitive ontology?

JLN: But once again, there is no question here... but an invitation to go further in this way. Of course I agree totally with you, maybe I could take up again from your point of arrival, this *entre-être*, not being between, but because *entre-être* in French, I feel, is better than in-between, since in being between we have once again the same between, being as a subject, and being without. It is all the time, the subject with a kind of predication. *Entre-être* makes quite a single word, it is no longer *être*, but *entre-être*, and I think it is maybe a way to go further in following Heidegger in the way of using to be

---

42. Is there not a platonism in a thinking of being as being-with? Does not being-with insist in promising a causality that at the end would hinder the opening towards a thinking of existence without reasons to be?

only as a verb, maybe as a *gérondif*, as you suggested, but I am afraid we cannot really use the gérondif in English, because «being» is already *solidifié* [solidified], like a noun. ‹To be›: in a purely verbal form, we can do nothing. It is the same in French with *être*, and German with *Sein*, there is nothing to be done with a pure verbal infinitive form. Maybe precisely this is what is called infinitive, there is no end, nothing is done with *être*. Maybe instead of Heidegger's suggestion to use it as a transitive verb in a non-grammatical usage that we can do nothing with – *être* cannot have any kind of complements – maybe we could try words like *entre-être*, or I would propose to add to *entre-être*, *plurrêtre* or *plus-être*. *Plurrêtre* is better, *plus-être* could be being-more, but *plurrêtre* is being-many. To understand that being is a quality of being belongs to the between, to the many… And then, together, that would be *avec-être*… but, I would say if we would be able to understand that to-be is a coming to existence, that is *ek-sister* – once again coming to Heidegger's *ek-sistens* – which precisely is not *existere*, it has no substance, no *substantia*, no instance, but ex-sistence, that can only be *inter- esse*, and *plurrêtre*, plural. Which is what I said yesterday, that it cannot be one thing, but is more than one, and if there are many things, the mere fact of existence is the putting apart of several things. And then there is the *entre* (the between). But if now we come back to the question of assemblage, togetherness, but together as a certain kind of order…

MCS:[43] On peut parler Français aussi, puisque la situation de notre séminaire est fatigante; c'est une situation de Babel, plusieurs langues à la fois dans chacun de nous et entre nous. C'est fatigant bien-sûr.

JLN: Oui, mais je ne sais pas ce que je veux dire ni en anglais, ni en français…Je ne sais pas quoi dire. C'est très difficile ça, parce que… it is a question of how to grasp the fact that the order is not given as a superior cause, it is not given as other form, by the order giver, not as an architect, but the order is given in a togetherness of things.

MCS: Est-ce qu'on pourrait parler d'une semiurgie?

JLN: Semiurgie, c'est-à-dire?

MCS: Semi, demi…

JLN: tu mélanges les langues…

MCS: Tout à fait, mais dans cette Babel où nous y sommes dans ce séminaire, on prononce un mot dans une langue et on l'entend en deux, c'est comme dit le psaume 61(60)

JLN: Un demi-oeuvre?

43. English translation on page 110.

MCS: Plutôt un entre-œuvre…

JLN: Bon, d'abord précisément, je me demande qu'est ce que c'est *Demiurgos*?

MCS: Le mot vient de demos, comme la Démocracie,…

JLN: Ça c'est un peut curieux…Demiurgos… [Nancy looks into his Greek dictionary]. Alors, «C'est l'homme que exerce le métier pour le publique». Voilà, tu as raison. Ah, mais c'est très intéressant! C'est magnifique!

MCS: Oui, Mais ça dépend de comment on comprend et entend le *Demos*. Est-ce qu'il faut comprend le *demos* d'après *l'ergon*, l'urgence de l'œuvre ou au contraire l'urgence de l'œuvre d'après le *demos*? Ou est-ce que cette alternative est mal placée? Parce que la difficulté, je pense, se trouve dans le vocabulaire demiourgique, dans la demiourgie du language est-elle-même, car en présentant la thèse du demiourge, Platon accomplit ce vice humain très humain de prendre le don et donné de la nature par un «fait», c'est'-à-dire par un oeuvre. Je pense ici à quelques mots de Valéry, qui se surprend de cette immédiate traduction du don par le fait. Il dit: «je regarde pour la première fois cette chose trouvée; j'y relève ce que j'ai dit, touchant sa forme, je m'en embarasse. C'est alors que je m'interroge: Qui donc a fait ceci? Mon premier mouvement d'esprit a été de songer au faire. L'idée de Faire est la première et la plus humaine »⁴⁴. Pour quoi, quand quelque chose nous arrive et, quand nous éprouvons l'étrange, la surprise de la vie elle même, on se pose la question du « faire », de l'œuvre? Pour quoi au lieu de simplement recevoir, on se place dans la perspective de l'avoir? Voici la génèse de la question de la cause, sa génèse disant artisanal, ce qui explique en partie pourquoi les mots du Demiurgos sont *cheiroplastés, tekton*... le fabricant qui produit des choses, des entités. Bien-sûr que tout le processus de la vie, des étants est là, mais l'image c'est de l'hypostasie, c'est ça qu'on voit le plus. C'est dans cette vision qui remplace le recevoir pour l'avoir qu'on perd immédiatement du vue l'être à venir, dans ce sens, mais il est là, bien sûr...

JLN: On le perd...moi je dirai qu'on ne le perd pas, mais qu'on le perd à partir du moment où on sépare l'image pour rester sur le terrain de l'image, c'est une bonne façon, comme tu l'avais dit tout à l'heure, d'approcher la question du fond, justement, parce que nous avons, c'est une habitude incroyablement ancienne et tenace dans la tradition occidental, de penser que il y a l'image et puis derrière il y a forcement un autre qui est le fond, à la fois le modèle, le fabricant de l'image, mais aussi la matière que supporte l'image, le subjectile[45] comme on dit en français, pour la matière sur laquelle

---

44. Paul Valéry, *Oeuvres*, Pléiade, vol. 1, p. 891.
45. In Littré Dictionnary, *subjectile* is defined as: « surface externe sur laquelle le peintre applique une couche d'enduit, de peinture, de vernis. Pour la première couche, le subjectile s'identifie au matéri-

on fait quelque chose, la toile, la matière, le bois, le marbre. Derrida a écrit un texte sur Artaud qui s'appelle *Forcener le subjectile*[46]. Alors, nous avons cette habitude, peut-être que l'une des différences le plus grandes entre notre culture et peut-être avec toutes les autres cultures du monde, ainsi comme la différence entre le sujet du mythe comme on avait parlé hier, c'est que dans toutes les autres cultures, l'image c'est justement la présentation de son propre fond. Un peu d'ailleurs comme l'*imago* en Latin qui avait aussi cette signification parce qu'il s'agissait des images des ancêtres. Je crois bien que les images des ancêtres ne voulaient pas être la représentation, la copie de l'ancêtre, une sorte de forme humaine, mais on disait ça été le grand-père, la grand-mère, et ces imagines ont été d'abord enfermées dans une sorte d'armoire sacré dans la maison et le patricien avait le droit de le sortir dans la rue à certains jours de fêtes. C' était un droit spécial appelé Jus imaginum, le droit de sortir ces images… Ce qui montre que l'imago latine est quelque chose de très religieux, si on veut un peu magique, c'est une présence, ce n'est pas de tout une représentation. Et je crois que pour nous les images

---

    au qui est appelé à recevoir le système de peintures». [External surface upon which the painter puts a layer of plaster, of painting, of varnish. For the first layer, the substrate is identified with the material which is required to receive the paint system.]
46. This word was used three times by Antonin Artaud in order to describe his own drawings. Jacques Derrida has discussed this expression in his *Forcener le subjectile* (Paris: Gallimard, 1986), English translation *To unsense the subjectile* (MIT, 1998).

de l'art, art en matière d'image ça veut dire ça, c'est à dire une image dont on ne cherche pas le fond derrière l'image. Par exemple, si on prend cette image [JLN montre une image publicitaire, un prospectus qui traîne sur la table pour une institution éducative] on comprend qu'il y a une intention de l'image, quelqu'un a inventé cette image, c'est une image illustrative, allégorique, parce que il s'agit de l'enfant, de la culture de l'enfant, on montre un enfant que est en train de jouer… Rien n'est dans l'image et tout est derrière, ailleurs. Mais si on prend une autre image, par exemple, l'Agnus Dei, l'agneau de Francisco Zurbarán, alors c'est tout autre chose, ce n'est pas la reproduction du tableau, mais le tableau lui-même, bien sûr on peut dire tout ce qu'on veut, qu'il renvoie à toute l'histoire chrétienne de l'agneau, qui est une histoire juive et chrétienne, le Nouveau Testament, l'agneau de Dieux sacrifié, etc. Mais qu'est qui est là, ce n'est pas ça, c'est la peinture extraordinairement précise, épais, c'est vraiment la laine du mouton, c'est beaucoup plus un affaire de toucher, et non plus de la représentation du toucher, c'est un toucher par et pour l'œil, ça met la laine dans l'œil. Donc, si on savait penser l'apparition du monde comme ça, c'est-à-dire, c'est à dire, là où tout est dans le paraître, et donc c'est que je voulais dire tout à l'heure, la venue du paraître, en fait on ne la perd peut-être pas, évidement, au même temps ça coupe la parole, parce que on peut dire, si je veux vraiment parler de cette laine du mouton, ça va être très difficile, progressivement, ça peut devenir aussi difficile que de parler de la musique.

On a parlé hier avec Peter de la musique, c'est un problème très particulier et très intéressant, la difficulté de parler de la musique. Il y a une sorte de ligne de bascule, entre trois discours, le discours musicologique, le discours allégorique et un discours indiscoursable de et sur la musique. Dans un concert pour clarinette de Mozart, la clarinette dialogue avec l'orchestre, il y a une histoire d'amour entre la clarinette et l'orchestre, oui! ça peut être très bien, très excitant, même pour les musiciens pour jouer, je cite quelqu'un qui est un très bon musicien, admirable, qui en train de faire répéter le concert pour clarinette, disait, «oh, il faut entendre, c'est un dialogue, c'est une histoire d'amour, ou... je ne sais pas quoi, de jalousie, de fâcherie...» alors, je me disait, c'est bien sûrement pour le musicien, mais c'est ne pas non plus la musique là, parce qu'on peut dire beaucoup des choses, que c'est l'amour, la haine,... Et donc à la limite, quand même, il y a une troisième partie, je ne sais pas très bien qu'est qu'on peut dire, on peut essayer de parler de pulsion, impulsion, de monter, de descendre, enveloppement et développement, beaucoup de choses, mais à la fin, on écoute la musique et c'est fini. Ou plutôt ça commence...

MCS: The experience of this difficulty of speaking about or rather from music is very important, I think, because, as you showed, it has to do with the fact that the sound is sounding before it begins and continues to sound when it finishes. It seems that you are suggesting that the phenomenality of music, its touching experience, is the real experience of history. Would you agree with that? In this sense, there is no loss of meaning or of ground, but.…? You said, there is no loss, but there is absence of meaning, but there is a without. How to distinguish loss and withoutness?[47]

On peut rappeler ici la différence entre les discours sur la Grèce et le commencement de la philosophie, tenu par Husserl et l'autre par Heidegger. Une grande différence c'est que Husserl assume qu'il y avait une Grèce philosophique originaire que s'était perdue de la modernité à cause de la naturalisation de la conscience, etc, pendant que pour Heidegger le commencement de la philosophie c'est la perte de la philosophie. Pour lui, le commencement est la perte.

JLN: Mais bien-sûr, Heidegger discute l'Occident comme un commencement par une perte. La perte du Pré-Socratique, la perte de l' émerveillement de l'être, après, c'est vrai, ça change.

MCS: Oui, mais je pense que ce tu disais est plus décisif. Si j'ai bien compris, tu voudrais nous rappeler que c'est important de quitter cette discursivité sur la perte dans le sens qu'on dit «ah, on ne peut plus jamais revenir», alors un peu dans le sens discuté [hier] par l'étudiant venu de la Turquie, qui disait que cette place où on n'arrive jamais, la Grèce, c'est la place ou plutôt c'est l'où on ne peut jamais revenir, mais

---

47. For an English translation of the following passage, see page 115ff.

qu'on ne peut la perdre non plus.⁴⁸ Ça serait aussi dire qu' il n'a pas un «loss of grounds», mais que cet «ground» is at the same time…, what is the contrary of loss, de la perte?

PARTICIPANT: Gain…

JLN: But there are two contraries, there is gain, but there is as well not loss. I wrote in my notebook: it is not lost, but it is not a gain. Gain is something that I receive, but…

MCS: Maybe we need to try to find another word for this. But at the same time the language, as you say, is what gives us in taking away from us – It gives us *la laine*, but in taking it away.

JLN: But it would not be a giving without the retreat of thinking by language or as language. Because, at the same time, language takes the thing in itself and then makes it unreal, and retreats itself, language itself retreats from itself and comes to silence. What happens with poetry? Poetry: every time I think of poetry, poetry itself comes to a certain end of talking and to a certain kind of silence, but silence as music, and not as muteness, not like when I press the mute button. But silence as a way of speaking beyond speech.

48. This part of the discussion from the day before was not recorded due to technical problems.

MCS: If I understood you correctly, we are saying that from within the experience of music as well as from within the experience of language in poetry, it is possible to distinguish between «having lost» and «being without». To remain close to Hölderlin, there is a short text that was maybe written by him, published in his complete works as «Zweifelhaftes», called *Communismus der Geister*[49]. It is a sketch for a dialogue between friends, discussing the loss of history, the relation with the disappearing of a great beginning. Hölderlin has doubts about the idea of having lost the origin, and speaks about «us», the moderns, as «Verbrecher vor der Geschichte», as «criminals in the face of history». What he says is ambiguous, for it is possible to interpret it so that we, the moderns, are criminals in the face of history because we can only relate to history as thieves longing for what we no longer possess. But we can understand his words in another sense, namely that we are criminals because, facing the «gap between here and there», «die Kluft zwischen hier und dort», we consider that we have lost what was beautiful and great. Indeed, he says at the end of this sketch that:

> I am not asking about what time has transmitted us, I am not asking about dead stuff but about the form in which time has happened, about the energy and con-

---

49. Friedrich Hölderlin, *Sämtliche Werke,* ed. Beissner, Grosse Stuttgarte Ausgabe, vol IV, p. 306-308.

sequences, that seem to lose themselves in infinity, so that what is most distant carries in itself the harmony with the middlepoint, sustaining in each variation the sound of the originary melody.⁵⁰

Hölderlin asks then: if we compare this time with ours where is a community to be found? Where are the bridges? You are saying, there are only bridges but not two different shores, the one that was lost and the other, the shore of having lost the other shore, aren't you? Or in other words – the crime we are comitting is the one of not listening to time and to the historical musically, and experiencing how the before can only appear afterwards, how time is contemporaneous in being a syncope to itself in itself⁵¹. In this sense, there is no loss of grounds, but the ground is a before that appears after a while, *nachträglich*, as melody, as a comet. «Not lost, but neither a gain». I understand this as without, as with-the-without, as *entre-être*, being-in-between.

May I continue a little more and follow this thread back

---

50. Ibidem, p. 308. [«Du verstehst mich, Ich frage nicht nach dem, was uns jenes Zeitalter überliefert hat, Ich frage nicht nach dem todten Stoffe, sondern, wenn du so willst, nach der Form in der es geschah, nach jener Energie und Consequenz, die sich in's Unendliche zu verlieren schien und demnoch auch in das Entfernste die Übereinstimmung mit dem Mittelpunkt trug, die in jeder Variation den Klang der ursprünglichen Melodie festhielt.»]
51. See Jean-Luc Nancy. *Le Discours de la syncope: I. Logodaedalus* (Paris: Flammarion, 1976), for the english version *The Discourse of the Syncope I, Logodaedalus* (California: Stanford Univeristy Press, 2008)

to the question of being-without and *entre-être*? I invented a dialogue for myself between you and Beckett, and especially with a short text written in French by Beckett with the title «Sans»[52]. He translated this text into English himself, and called it «Lessness». Cioran discussed with him how the English title was so much better than the French one. The text is composed of 120 sentences, and the 61st and 62nd are a kind of *reflexive mirror*, a kind of polyphony, in which he aimed to sound as if six voices were sounding at the same time, to show the small displacements of this ‹putting-together›, to show this putting together in a paratactical, not a syntactical way, and so, in this sense, without ground. He wrote there:

> Ruines vrai refuge enfin vers lequel d'aussi loin par tant de faux. Lointains sans fin terre ciel confondus pas un bruit rien qui bouge. Face grise deux bleu pâle petit corps coeur battant seul debout. Eteint ouvert quatre pans à la renverse vrai refuge sans issue.
>
> Ruines répandues confondues avec le sable gris cendre vrai refuge. Cube tout lumière blancheur rase faces sans trace aucun souvenir. Jamais ne fut qu'air gris sans temps chimère lumière qui passe...[53]

52. Samuel Beckett. *Sans*, (Paris: Editions de Minuit, 1969). La traduction de Beckett sous le titre *Lessness* a été completé à l'Académie der Künste et publié pour la première fois à New Statesman (1/5/70).
53. Ruins true refuge long last towards which so many false time out of mind. All sides endlessness earth sky as one no sound no stir. Grey face two pale blue little body heart beating only up right. Blacked

Everything here is paratactical. He uses the word ‹sans›, less, in expressions such as without time, without issue, so timeless, issueless, etc. The text speaks all the time about there being no way out of the world, of how *la terre et ciel* are mixed, how they are a reflex of their being a reflex. In this short text, we can find a *poétique du céleste*, a celestial poetics, where the being together, one and another, is described as one becoming the other when the other becomes itself another, disappearing for itself. It is a kind of *Werden im Vergehen*, a «devenir dans le périssable [becoming in dissolution]», to use another title by Hölderlin. Beckett does not say «devenir dans le périssable ou dissolution»[54] mais il le pense et pour le dire il use plutôt le mot «reflux», comme par exemple, dans le vers: «Encore le dernier reflux, le gallé mort, le demi tour pouis le part vers le vielle lumière». Dans ce texte sur le Lessness, Le sans, qui est pour lui «le sens», Beckett ne parle pas sur «loss» nor of «absence» of grounds and fonds – il parle d'un se faisant en se défaisant, il parle je pense d'un geróndif, d'un nom, le nom est «l'inominable». Ma question serait donc si le discours sur le «loss of grounds», le titre de notre project, qui a comme point de départ «l'absence du fondement», l'Abgründigkeit, n'est

> out fallen open four walls over backwards true refuge issueless.
> Scattered ruins same grey as the sand ash grey true refuge. Four square all light sheer white blank planes all gone from mind. Never was but grey air timeless no sound figment the passing light. No sound no stir ash grey sky mirrored earth mirrored sky. Never but this changelessness dream the passing hour.

54. English translation on page 116ff.

toujours encore une fondamentalisation de l'être? Formulé autrement, est-ce qu'il y a une différence entre «loss», «absence» et le «sans», le «lessness»? Il me sembe que le «loss», «l'absence» dit tout le temps, «after» le fondement, «after» the subject, «after» the wall, que ces expressions produisent un «after-ism», que renforce la logique du fondement, la logique fondationelle qui recouvre à nouveau l'existence jetée, le sens qui a du sens sans raison d'être. The absence of ground is in a certain way a new ground and then we are again entangled in the Logos of the ground. Dans le «after-ism» d'un discours sur le «loss», sur «l'absence», la question du «mais quoi faire», «what should be done?» ne cesse de se reprocesser. Mais dans le «sans», entrevu par Beckett, il semble que le non-way out de l'existence montre le reflux de l'existence, l'existence comme reflux, un se faisant en se défaisant, un «ruisseau qu'on devine à peine», comme disait aussi Hölderlin, un «à peine» deviner d'une petite ouverture que est quasiment une petite clairère, «chimère, lumière», something that I think you are thinking all the time, but that sounds clearer to me when you named *entre-être*, between-being, I think.

JLN: I'll start with this... *Werden im Vergehen*. Ce que Hölderlin a en vue, si je me souviens un peu du texte, c'est le passage du fini à l'infini. Le fini devient, devenant il va vers sa fin, et dans sa fin il passe à l'infini. Il ne «devient» pas infini, c'est là le point important: il s'ouvre infiniment. La finitude épuisée indique l'advenue souveraine de l'infini...

«Je» ne m'infinitise pas, au contraire. Mais «je» en se taisant indique... tout...[55]

There is a wonderful sentence of Bataille: «*Seul le language indique, à la limite, le moment souverain où il n'a plus cours*». This is in the End of Eroticism. «Only language reveals, at the limit, the sovereign moment, when it no longer has any currency. But in the end the one who speaks owns up to his impotence»[56]. «*Avoir cours*», to have currency, that is, le Euro a cours, has currency. I can pay with Euro... Avoir cours is maybe not only for money, but mainly for money. If I go to China, Euro is not the currency, but it is full of value in the computer of the Chinese, but in the street, il n'a pas cours. Currency is in the same family of the word cours, to circulate. Language indicates itself the souverain point where it is no longer used.

IS: Or it cannot be exchanged, maybe...for something else...

JLN: Yes, it cannot be exchanged...

---

55. What Hölderlin has in view, if I recall some of the text, is the passage from the finite to the infinite. The finite becomes, and becoming it goes to its end, and in its end, it enters infinity. It does not «become» infinite, and this is the important point: it opens infinitely. Exhausted finitude indicates the sovereign event of infinity ... «I» do not infinitise myself, on the contrary. But the silencing of the «I» says everything ...
56. Georges Bataille. *L'Erotisme* (Paris: ed. de Minuit, 1957), eng version *Erotism: Death and Sensuality: a study of eroticism and of the Taboo* (NY: Walker and Company, 1962)

MCS: It goes back to the question of communication...

JLN: Precisely this is the point where language has no value. It is at the same time the point where one can no longer speak and maybe the point where one may speak but no longer with an exchange value. This is precisely the point of poetry. Or in another way...

KRYSTOF KASPRZAK: In the sense of expression and not communication...

JLN: Yes, but ‹expression›...what does that mean?

PARTICIPANT: Expression can be part of communication...

IS: Yes, but not in general, perhaps in the sense indicated by Benjamim, when language becomes all expression and therefore «sovereign». And that means it cannot be exchanged for something else.

JLN: But what does expression mean? It does not mean signification of some internal status. It means... maybe we could say it means almost the same as a presentation of the thing itself, not signification, not representation, but presentation. In a way, the *mouton*, the sheep, is in the word sheep, it is not the signified of the signifier, but it is a word, mouton or sheep. And precisely in English, for example, there is sheep and lamb. Sheep is the living animal and lamb is food. We don't have two words in French.

JLN: Why do you think that expression is the word in which this appears?

KK: It just came to my mind when you were talking about Benjamin, that the sense of expression is not even presentation, but rather appearing.

JLN: Exactly, and so, this is why the question of language is so close to the question of the appearing of the world. I think that it is something that is quite difficult to express in the ordinary sense of communication. Man and language, no: man is language. First, man is not absolutely alone and apart from the rest of the world; but it does not mean that man speaks like dolphins and bees, etc, that is, communicating. What is special is that we are absolutely unable, that there is no expression for, for instance, the beauty of the colors of flowers. The beautiful colors of flowers, of birds, in a way, the beautiful colors of everything, the color of the sea under the sun at the end of the day, you know, Rimbaud's *L'eternité de la mer, allée avec le Soleil*. What are colors, if something else than a spectrum of colours, remaining on the side of Goethe against Newton and Hegel. Color is something else than a physical phenomenon. A young philosopher, Claude Romano, wrote a good book about color, not exactly a book, but a seminar on color, which is now published[57], very interesting, because his conclusion is that color is primarily a phenomenological datum. And he has nothing more to say than that color belongs to, precisely, the appearing of the world. Nothing appears without color, as Toussaint[58], the French painter, said once, nothing visible is given without lines and colors. But precisely color is like a repetition of what we can imagine as the first appearing of the world. Many things and many colors, and we could say color is nothing else but the diversity of colors. The spectrum is the same in a way, but as decomposition of light in colors. But that is the point of view of Newton, maybe you are looking at this from that point of view. But the point of view of Goethe (and of the artist, too) is the feeling that it is at the same time, in the first place, the great, great, infinite diversity of colors, and secondly, that each color is unique. It is grey here, this red near you is unique. And as Wittgenstein writes, if I show a point of blue in a canvas and I say, I need my room to be painted with this blue, it is almost impossible, because that blue in the canvas cannot be taken and reproduced and extended to another place, because it is that blue only at this place. But now I have taken another direction, different from the first one. My first direction was to say that the color is not something like, self-expression of ... Nature? Things. I wanted to say first that language is not

57. Claude Romano. *De la couleur* (Chatou: Les editions de la transparence, 2010)
58. Nicolas-Toussaint Charlet, see, far example, *Le jour ni l'heure*.

alone, language belongs to a universal function, of what? Of expressing things one to another. Colors, sounds, all sensibility or sensible, if you prefer – as you say, sensibility is too Jane Austen [laughter in the room].

MCS: But that's OK [more laughter].

JLN: It is ok with Jane Austen? But, second, the proper difference of language is that language expresses this expression as such, for itself. And then, the function of communication which implies a signification and the play of signs, *le fait de renvoyer à autre chose, significant, signifié et référant* [the fact of referring to something else, signifier, signified and referent]. The function of communication is only there to allow that the function of expression... but the function of the expression goes the same way, that is, faire un renvoie a un signifié, mais il n'y a pas de référant. C'est le renvoi du langage à lui même. Et alors c'est aussi pourquoi le renvoie peut être un renvoie au silence, mais aussi bien au mot lui même [59].

MCS: Comme un «reflux» de Beckett? [Like the reflux in Beckett?].

JLN: Un «reflux», oui, si tu veus, oui... [A reflux, yes, if you

---

59. One refers to a signified, but there is no referent. At stake here is the reference of language to language itself. And so that's why the reference can both be a reference to silence, and to the word itself.

want...]. Therefore, I would like to be able to say that man and language are given in the world – to the world – in order precisely to manifest, to make manifest the manifestation of everything to everything, or to manifest the world as such. This is to say, with Kant, that man is the goal of nature, but at the same time this goal is not the goal as if Nature would achieve itself there, going I don't know where, to the modern world... As Kant says, but in a way I would say that maybe it is true that man and language are there, are the goal of Nature, Nature trying to express itself and having nothing else to do than express itself. Then, we could say that man and language are myth in Schelling's meaning, as the tautegory of being.

MCS: Myth as «Lichtblick des Seins» (as he says in the Freedom essay).

JLN: Aha...

MCS: This is an interesting expression, very difficult to translate. In saying «*Lichtblick*», what is being said, I think, is that man is not a goal, but the place, the scene, the *Bühne*, where the becoming of being, or the appearing as such appears. Comment comprendre l'homme comme la scène, comme le mirroir où se donne le «*Lichtblick des Seyns*» ?[60] Hölderlin a dit

60. How can we understand man as the scene, as the mirror in which the «Lichtblick des Seyns», the light-gaze of being takes place? Hölderlin said that the question of who man is should be adressed

qu'il fallait tourner la question de qui est l'homme vers le ciel, car du ciel il devient possible de voir la terre «sonnante comme la peau de veau tendue», «tönend, wie des Kalbs Haupt, die Erde»[61]. Comment poser cette question au ciel? Dans quelle langue? What would be the perspective from which we can think that and if you ask the heavens, what kind of perspective is to be thought? Because we cannot put ourselves in another place than this place. I don't know... How can we think that, how this question is possible? Or not.

JLN: Maybe it is possible because from this place, our place, when we look to the heavens, I would say, precisely we know we are not only in the phenomenological position, that is, not only a subject looking at an object, but that we are looked at, we are considered by the heavens themselves. To consider is to be with the stars, ‹con-siderare›, is ‹de-siderium›, it is supposed to be without being far from the stars. But why do we think that the stars are looking at us? At least we know one thing, that the question starts with animals: what is the gaze of an animal upon me? Derrida developed that, starting from the gaze of his cat looking at him naked. It is a text which has

---

to the sky, because from the sky it becomes possible to see the earth «Ringing out on the calf's hide», «tönend, wie des Kalbs Haupt, Die Erde «. How to put this question to the sky? In what language?

[61]. Hölderlin, Griechenland, 3 Version, ed. Beissner, op. cit, vol. 1, p. 179; en français, par Gustav Roude, op. Cit. P. 917. In English, trans. M. Hamburger, »Ringing out on the calf's hide», in *Friedrich Hölderlin, Poems and Fragments* (London: Anvil Press, 2005), p. 699.

now became an entire book, the animal which I am, *L'animal que donc je suis*.⁶² I think he explains something about that, I don't know, I don't quite remember, but the «therefore» is the conclusion of the thinking about me, about our place. The question of the animal has been very important in France, at least in the last 20 years, so to say, but mainly, not only in Derrida but maybe even more in Deleuze. Precisely, Deleuze is very correct to say ‹don't take the animal as part of human world, but let it be the animal in the animal world›. But where is the animal world? It is from this world we are looking at it. With a cat or a dog, or with horses it is clearer. That is the reason I was saying yesterday, I think we should be able to invent a new philosophy of nature. Or maybe I am wrong, maybe it is precisely a philosophy *of* nature that is no longer the task we have. Maybe we have, I don't know… at least there is no longer nature, all is technique.

KK: But is it really Nature which is the problem, or is it that ‹of›, that is the problem (in philosophy *of* nature)?

JLN: Ah, yes, you are right. Both, I would say both. Because there is a philosophy of…

---

62. Jacques Derrida. *L'animal que donc je suis* (Paris: Gallilée, 2006) the last book by Derrida, published posthumously. This book was edited by Marie Louise Mallet based on texts and recording from his lectures at Cerisy. Translated into English by David Wills as *The Animal That Therefore I Am* (New York: Fordham University Press, 2008).

KK: Because the problem with nature is that we are incapable of thinking it otherwise than through this ‹of›. There is a distance...

JLN: With the philosophy of nature we were, like Hegel, Schelling, able to give to nature – to take *from* nature, in a certain way – a lot, a lot of signification that is partly symbolic (partly... or maybe everything was symbolic). Nature as belonging to the complete order of something that Hegel calls *Geist*, Spirit. And then Hegel is able to say that the light is this and that (this is wonderful in Hegel, the light, the shadow and the place, the gravity, life, birds, everything is there...). What makes the ‹of› there is that all this signified Nature is attributed to the spirit. It is the life of spirit, so spirit becomes itself nature but through the becoming of nature, it becomes, after, that spirit, it becomes man, language, philosophy, and all comes back to the first time, and the first time, at the end we discover that the first time was already the spirit in its total self-sufficiency in a certain way. When we ask about *Ungrund*, it is as if we would ask the same thing as Hegel, only without the spirit, if you want.

KK: Would you see Schelling as an opening, in contrast to Hegel, in which Nature could appear as the divisible of spirit, and the spirit as the indivisible of nature, not a concrete fulfilment but...?

JLN: You are right, I don't know enough Schelling, but I have the feeling it would be more or less the same as Hegel. Something is always already given to us, the spiritual principle of the world, or of everything. We are in a condition in which it is as if we should really start with nothing. And not replacing any kind of spirit or [something] already given in one world, in one God. This is the meaning of the *l'être* of God, nothing more than that. God is dead, everything is there and nothing is lost.

IS: I would like to come back to Marcia's question about the urgency of asking the heavens and the subject of con-sideration. But what kind of heaven would it be if we don't have grounds? Is there any heaven if there are no grounds? Democracy, for instance, does democracy have a Heaven?

JLN: You know why, when I was talking about Heaven I was confusing Heaven and sky. Because in French it is the same word. [...] Heaven means *salut*. To me, the best way out of salvation is the phrase of Derrida, we talked about this yesterday, the phrase of Derrida at the end of the book *Le toucher, Jean-Luc Nancy*, when he comes to the idea of salvation and precisely because he is expecting me to be a hidden Christian... no, that is true, all the time he thought this about me, and he writes this in *Le Toucher* in a certain way, but it was more explicitly when he was talking directly to me, «you cannot deconstruct Christianity because it will always remain Christianity at the end.»

All the time you rest at the «cœur» of Cristianity. Through this suspicion, he came to something strong, I find: he says «*un salut sans salvation* [to salute without salvation]», *salvation* is a very unusual word in French. *Salut sans salvation*, that is, *le salut qu'on dit en Français*, ‹*salut*› [To salute without salvation, that is, the meaning of the French ‹salut›]. – Hello. This is, at the same time, used for coming and for going. *Salut! Salut!* This *salut*, I could add to what Derrida says, has a certain kind of *Wink*. *Wink* is this German untranslatable word, although it seems it can be said in Portuguese...

MCS: Yes, we have the beautiful word *aceno*, that has in itself the word *cena*, the scene.

JLN: Yes, some Portuguese people told me that, and I think it is now written somewhere, *Wink* in German is a sign, it can be a sign with a *clin d'oeil*, it can be mainly in the German ordinary life, it is mainly what small children are supposed to do because they don't speak very well, so they do «*Winke, Winke*».

TL: En Suédois on dit aussi, ‹*vinka*›, ‹*vinka*›.

JLN: En français on n'arrive pas à traduire *Wink*. Parce -que signe c'est un signe sans signification, ou plutôt avec une signification trop large et imprecise. *Wink*, alors c'est comme salut, un peu comme *Hello*, it is mixed with something with signification, like good day, good evening, but without the explicit signification of good, that is a signification of salvation or health, etc. Without the Roman *salve*, the Greek *khaire*, good chance, *salut* has something of that. And I like that because, I would say color is a kind of *salut*. And of course it can become something more, because it is something else, like a signal in an appeal, sex appeal for instance (for birds color plays frequently a role in the sexual attraction, the same happens with other animals; but with the flower, I don't know, I've never heard of that... or maybe for the bees). Color, sounds, finally that would be the question: what exactly is the sensual, or sensibility, or sensitivity if you prefer? What is it? It is an organization of information, an exchange of information, it is communication or expression, one could say, that can be the question. Or is it sensitivity precisely a kind of language, of language as communication, or something else? And I am sure that if we re-read precisely what Hegel says about color, maybe it would be something else than we have expected, color is not necessarily a step for the self manifestation of *Geist*. Of course it is, I can't say this *a priori*, but maybe it is at the same time something which does not belong to the final achievement as a first step... parce que peut-être dans toute la philosophie de la nature de Hegel il y a de choses, des elements, des stades, ce'st toujours la question du stade, comme j'ai dit hier sur Freud. Il y a des stades qui ne sont pas seulement depassés et relevés à la fin, mais qui sont là. Comme l'enfant, mais oui, c'est vous qui avez parlé de l'enfant... Comme chez Marx, il y a chez lui un seul passage en faveur de l'enfance, mais qui est très étrange, car elle se réfère à la place de l'art today.[63] Marx says that we have no longer need of myth, like Prometheus, because we are walking with irons, walking by ourselves, because we have the telegraph.[64] He says, the myths are dead in a way, nevertheless he writes, we are still touched by Greek works of art, because they are for us, like something belonging to childhood[65]. The text I

63. Hegel because perhaps in Hegel's whole philosophy of nature there are things, elements, stages, and it is always a question of stages, as I said in relation to Freud yesterday. There are stages that are not only surpassed and sublated at the end, but that remain there. Like the child, but yes, it was you who talked about the child (turning to Victoria Fareld)... As in Marx, we find in Marx one single passage in favor of the children, very strange one indeed because it refers to the place of art...
64. A la fin de l' «Introduction générale» de 1857 qui se trouve dans les *Grundrisse* (Marx-Lenin-Institut, Dietz Verlag Berlin, 1953), p. 30-31.
65. See Karl Marx, *Grundrisse*, translated into English by Martin Nicolaus, 1973, Penguin Books, at the end of the Introduction: «But the difficulty lies not in understanding that the Greek arts and epic are bound up with certain forms of social development. The difficulty is that they still afford us artistic pleasure and that in a certain respect they count as a norm and as un unattainable model. A man cannot become a child again, or he becomes childish. But does he not find joy in the child's naîveté, and must he himself not strive to reproduce its truth at a higher stage? Does not the true character of each epoch come alive in the nature of its children? Why should not the historic childhood of humanity, its most beautiful unfolding, as a stage never to return, exercise an eternal charm? There are unruly children and precocious children. Many of the old peoples belong in this category. The Greeks were normal children. The charm of their art for us is not in contradiction to the undeveloped stage of society on which it grew. [It] is its result, rather, and is inextricably bound up, rather, with the fact that the unripe social conditions under-

think is ‹still new›, each moment new, and childhood would be what is the new, being ever new.

MCS: I wish we could continue to talk with you and listen to you without end. But we have already taken too much of your hospitality. I think there wouldn't be a better way to interrupt our conversation than with the thought of «being ever new», of a «still new» belonging to childhood. How could we thank you, Jean-Luc Nancy for everything you gave us these two days, for the «still and ever new» of your thoughts, for your *accueil*, (yours and Helene's) for the sushi, *du riz et du sourire*? We arrived with some withouts and you opened your home and time to be with our withouts!

which it arose, and could alone arise, can never return».

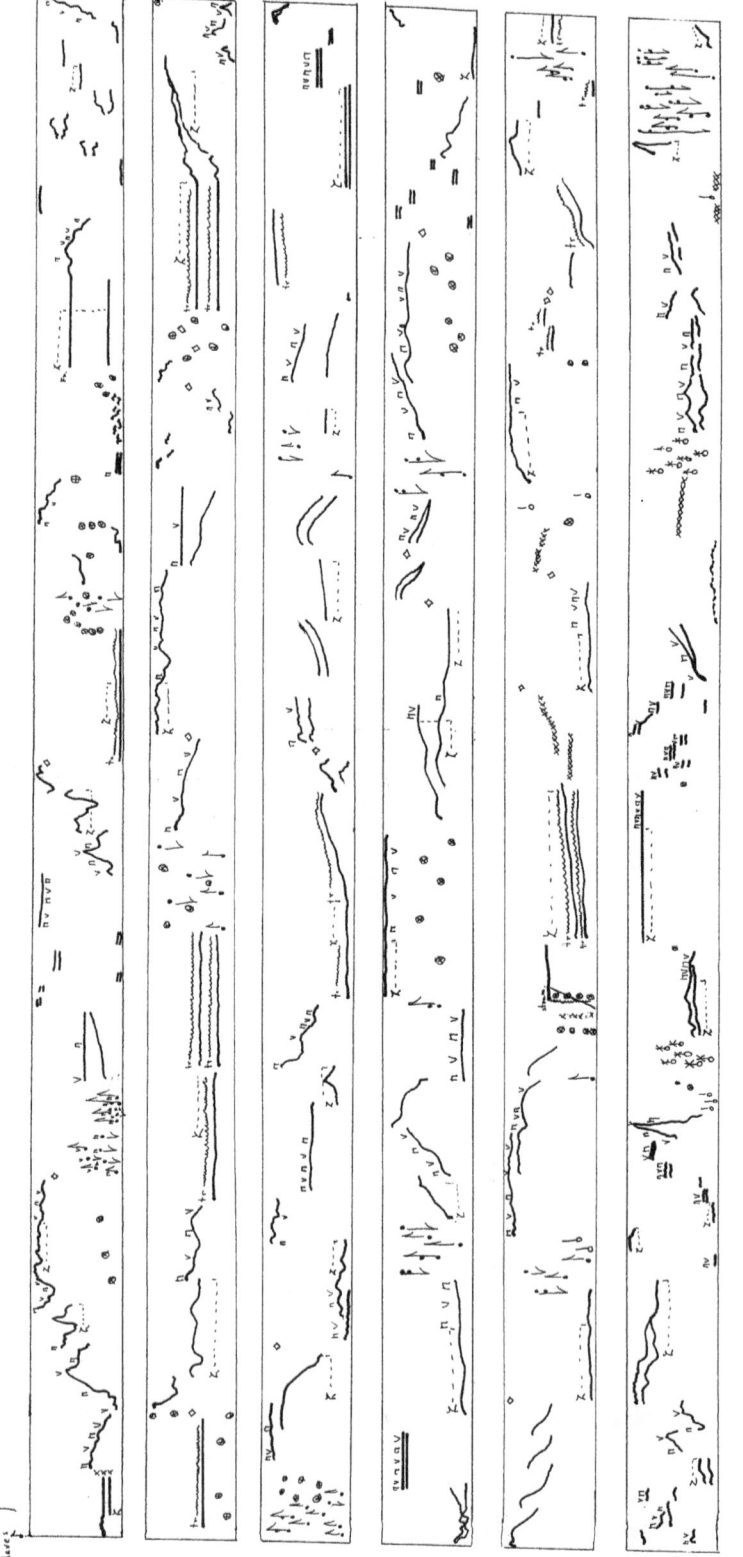

Post Scriptum

Absence: un hommage à Jean-Luc Nancy

PETER SCHUBACK:[66] Le temps et la mémoire sont probablement les principaux éléments relatifs à la pensée d'un musicien, si on peut appeler ça une pensée ou s'il s'agit d'un itinéraire actif pour dissoudre la présence. Pour un musicien, les pensées circulent auprès du temps présent à la recherche d'un rapport plus éthérique à l'absence. On peut se demander si la mémoire se souvient de l'absence ou de la présence. Est-ce que la mémoire peut avoir une mémoire de la mémoire? Une réponse à cette question ne se trouve que dans l'écoute où tous ces paramètres coïncident et se dissolvent simultanément par leurs propres existences. L'écoute de l'absence nous fait écouter la présence. Ma pièce *Absence* de 1975 a été écrite pour travailler cette question. Le titre aussi bien que le contenu versent sur les circuits de la mémoire. Le souvenir de ce que nous avons écouté et la mémoire de ce que nous savons que nous allons écouter. Nous trouvons d'innombrables événements sonores. Dans l'absence une

66. English translation on page 118.

présence émerge. La relation entre les deux apporte une extension de la mémoire de l'absence et le raccourcissement de la mémoire dans la présence. Peut-être que c'est ici que la musique présente l'écart entre l'écrit et la performance du tel ou tel donné à chaque instant, de l'improvisé. Dans l'improvisation, il se passe justement ça, la mémoire nous rappelle l'avenir et nous faire quitter le passé par la présence de l' absence.

Concernant la visite à Jean-Luc Nancy à Strasbourg, je suis allé comme accompagnant et pas comme membre du groupe de recherche. Il était important ou plutôt correct de me tenir à distance des discussions académiques qui, certes, m'ont apporté beaucoup de joie. La mémoire semblait tout le temps comme le centre de tout ce que j'ai entendu. Il s'agissait autant de la mémoire de l'avenir comme de la mémoire du passé. J'étais donc à la fois absent et présent.

Le dernier jour, lorsque le groupe s'est réuni chez Jean-Luc Nancy, dont j'avais déjà fait la connaissance à Saint-Pétersbourg, où nous avons passé deux jours ensembles, il m'a posé une question concernant la musique et la lecture de partitions. Ma réponse a semblé assez surprenante parce que j'ai dit qu'en regardant une partition la notation se voit mais ne s'entend pas. Avec cette question il est devenu impossible pour moi de ne pas participer à la discussion générale. Mais comme la discussion a lentement changé de cours, elle s'est évanoui peu à peu. Présence par l'absence.

Mon oeuvre *Absence*, traite de la mémoire d'un temps, de la mémoire tant de l'absence comme de la présence, de la mémoire de l'improvisation. Comme instrument j'ai choisit l'alto, qui le plus exprime la solitude. Dans sa construction, il est le plus proche de mon instrument, le violoncelle, mais dans son esprit peut-être le plus loin. En fait ce n'est que dans la proximité que l'absence peut se développer. L'oeuvre est pour moi aujourd'hui comme un cahier de mémoire d'un temps qui s'est révélé à nouveau pour moi à travers cette visite à Jean-Luc Nancy. L'oeuvre s'est donc refait par sa présence.

Afterword

After our visit, after working with this mosaic, a short poem by Rilke came continuously to my mind. If I were Rilke, I would have dedicated these verses to Jean-Luc Nancy:

> Aufgesetzt auf den Bergen des Herzens. Siehe, wie klein dort,
> siehe: die letzte Ortschaft der Worte, und höher,
> aber wie klein auch, noch ein letztes
> Gehöft und Gefühl. Erkennst du's?
> Ausgesetzt auf den Bergen des Herzens. Steingrund
> under den Händen. Hier blünt wohl einiges auf; aus stummen Absturz
> blüht ein unwissendes Kraut singend hervor.
> Aber der Wissende? Ach, der zu wissen begann
> und schweigt nun, ausgesetzt auf den Bergen des Herzens.
> Da geht wohl, heilen Bewusstseins,
> manches umher, manches gesicherte Bergtier,
> wechselt und weilt. Un der grosse geborgene Vogel
> kreist um der Gipfel reine Verweigerung – Aber
> ungeborgen, hier auf den Bergen des Herzens...[67]

---

67. Written at Irchenhauser, September, 1914. English translation on page 120.

To Jean-Luc Nancy, le penseur exposé à la montagne du cœur, this rhopographical mosaic, gathering the small pieces that remained from this beautiful feast you made possible.

Merci,

MCS au nom du groupe suédois
Stockholm, Octobre 2012

Translations

To page 51ff.

I would like to pursue this insistence upon the question of *être avec*, *Mitsein*, being-with; more precisely the question concerning the connection between being-with and being-without, to the degree that one could describe this experience of being-with as a kind way of living in a condition of being fundamentally *without: Ohnesein, être sans*; and in an extension of this reflection that would pose the question of how to articulate being-with as precisely an experience of a being-without at the core of a corporeal ontology.

To give you the context of my question: in my doctoral work I was interested in the question of ‹recognition› – *Annerkung/ reconnaissance*. What interested me was a certain schizophrenia at the heart of the political debate about recognition: even if the discussion about the desire for recognition revolved around the constitutive dependence upon others as the foundation of our existence, it nonetheless reproduces an ideal of autonomy and independence, throughout the community.

In other words, recognition is treated solely as an appropriative force, through which one achieves access to oneself by way of others, and not as an *ex*propriative force which would rather signal a loss – a constitutive, originary loss – precisely of the connection *between* self and possesion. In this work, I tried to find a different way of speaking about recognition, one that would take its ex-propriative force as point of departure.

OK, so…in my current work, I wanted to continue to explore philosophical resources for the thematization of the experience of exposure, of expropriation, of the fundamental dependence and vulnerability at the basis of our existence, our *co*-existence. Even if I have left behind the question of recognition, my concerns remain, one might say, with half of the word *reconnaissance*: I remain concerned with the second part of the word: with *naissance*, birth.

One experience that is very concrete – perhaps even too much so – of ‹coming into being, or into co-existence›, would be *birth*. It is highly symptomatic that the history of philosophy has demonstrated so little interest, in the end, in experiences connected with birth, and with infancy (with, of course, certain notable exceptions). What has determined the tone has been rather more the idea that these experiences of dependence, of the exposure and vulnerability connected with birth and infancy are merely stages to be overcome.

In the *Discourse on Method*, Descartes expresses regret that man is not born adult. Childhoood, infancy, represents a state of lack or insufficiency. To become adult is to declare one's independence (following Kant): *Selbständigke*it, self-sufficiency in the original sense of the word – *selber, aus eigener Kraft stehen können*, to be able to stand up through one's own strength.

This ‹adultocentrism›, which is so present in the history of philosophy indicates, I find, a resistance to the acceptance of exposure – even the exposure which allows the sense of connection, of co-existence that makes us possible. We are – and not only in birth or in childhood – we remain fundamentally dependent on that which is outside of us in order that our lives be liveable: our bodies are exposed to injury, to sickness, cold, heat, to hunger, thirst, love, desire.

In your thinking, I find a language within this language that can express the constitutive ideas of being-with as, precisely, a *being-without*. *Being-with* indicates a mode of being-in-common without commonality, a community *without* totality. As you write in *L'Expérience de la liberté*: «with no connection at all, and in this itself thrown into connection», we share something which we do not have; expressed by you in a poetic way: «we are separated by that which binds us».

So then, at the basis of our co-existence, our *Mitsein*, there is *Ohnesein* in the sense of being-without, but also in the sense of «without-being»; in the sense of the withdrawal of being in the face of a connecting; of being that draws back in giving that connection: being-*with*, *Mitsein*; or perhaps a ‹*between*-being›.

So, in effect, the *with* reveals the *without* – the without-commonality. Love, the sexual act, orgasm express this impossibility of being-in-common. However, the event which marks, perhaps the most violently, this impossibility is, I would like to say, *birth*. Birth is a moment which allows for the experiencing of coexistentiality, the being-with, as – precisely – a mode of being-without.

The two bodies which separate (in the very instant of separation that is the moment of birth) enter into relation; into a between-being, in effect. I think that birth as a philosophical question would enable us to think the being-without (*l'être sans* in close proximity to an *être sens* – with an e) as the ground without ground of being-with, if you wish, in affirming the exteriority of the body – of enormous importance – of the body as finite and plural.

I think it is important to try to find a language within language, a position that would allow for the expression or the thought of the corporeal – the corpo-real, perhaps – of between-being.

At the same time, I hesitate. What would this mean? A corporeal ontology of coexistence that would take as its point of departure exposure, vulnerability, dependence, and which would allow us to articulate the experience of being-without at the core of our existence; an ontology that would, at the same time, of necessity be a social and political ontology (bodily being is at the same time a being-exposed to social and political forces; in being a «human» body, one cannot exist outside of its political and social organization).

What I would love to discuss with you is in the first place

the idea of even wanting to take as a point of departure for philosophical (or lets say political) reflection not reason, and not sociality or the finitude of man, but rather an absolute dependence on a between-being. What would be the ethical demand of such a project?

And what would be its dangers – knowing that ‹vulnerability›, ‹fragility›, ‹exposure› have become key words in a contemporary political vocabulary of ‹prevention›, of a ‹security industry› through which we are presented as ‹exposed to the other›, exposed to threats which come from outside us. But equally, on a more philosophical level: what would it mean to place this idea of a *being-without* at the heart of being-with as the foundation of a reflection – of an ontology, ultimately?

To page 56ff.

I entirely agree. I would just remind you that Hannah Arendt herself accords a privilege to birth, to «natality». In French, this word designates rather «birth-rate» of a population, as indeeed does «mortality» although the latter can also be understood as the «characteristic of being mortal». And Arendt wishes to speak of a characteristic of being «nascent», «natal», a «towards birth», as you wish. For her, this is the real value of beginning, of innovation. I don't want to dwell on her, we would need her texts for this. But I emphasize the following: Arendt certainly thought this natality in counterpoint to Heidegger's «being-toward-death». Being – or a being – which is born is as alone in birth as it is in death. As alone, and also as «with» (because I do think that death is also a «with», despite everything). Principally «with», even – and this is what you said» to be born, to separate, to individuate, to enter into relation. And as Freud says, we are being born throughout our lives. All the time we are beginning again this relation, relations, connections, leave-takings and returns, we receive and we approach...

For my part, however, I would not insist on vulnerability and dependence: these are modes of speaking that lean more or less consciously on the image of the autonomous individual – complete and self-sufficient – as if, deep down, that is what he *must be*. And today, it is in the name of this figure that the pattern of «care» proliferates, of caring and taking care...of course we must take care, because we have to. But is not true care a remitting of the other towards his own (re)birth? (In saying this, I am in fact paraphrasing a passage from Heidegger on «*Fürsorge*»). Is it not a «Go! Begin again!»? For example, a good doctor is one who knows how to «leave» the sick person, to allow him to return to ordinary life, with its risks, its uncertainties, and even with the possibility that the sickness might regain strength...if care invades life, it no longer cares. On the contrary, it is necessary for care to renounce itself.

«Exposure» is not «vulnerability», it is ex-istence,

ek-sistence. As you say, we are in a society of maximal security...and we understand even this as a danger! Exposure is exposure to a *without* which is at the heart of the «with»....

To page 59ff.

MCS: On the way to Strasbourg we made a small detour to Hölderlin's tower in Tübingen. We arrived at Karlsruhe and started our journey to you passing by Hölderlin, through the solitude of Hölderlin, to begin this walking journey on the soil of poetry. Hölderlin wrote a poem called *Der Spaziergang*, The promenade, where we find the following verses:

> Ihr lieblichen Bilder im Tale,
> Zum Beispiel Garten und Baum,
> Und dann der Steg, der schmale,
> Der Bach zu sehen kaum

> Ô jolies images du val,
> Arbres et jardins, par exemple,
> Et puis ce sentier très étroit,
> Le ruisseau qu'on devine à peine.

> You graceful views in the valley,
> For instance garden and tree
> And then the footbridge, the narrow,

The stream one can hardly see

These images, trees and gardens – «for instance», «zum Beispiel», i.e. which play in proximity – we pass by so many images, in the streets, in books, in thought, and then we see the narrow path, the creek we can barely make out – I am taking these verses as an epigraph of our trip, our journey to you, because the sense of the without that haunts us seems still confined, hard to make out, amid so many thought-images.

To page 68ff.

MCS: We can talk in French, since the situation of our seminar is a tiring one; it is a Babel-like situation: several languages at the same time, between and inside each of us. It is tiring, of course.

JLN: Yes, but I don't know what I want to say, either in English or in French, I don't know what to say. This is not easy, because...

MCS: Could one speak here of *semiurgy*?

JLN: Semiurgy, meaning?

MCS: Semi-, demi-, half- ...

JLN: You are mixing languages...

MCS: Absolutely, but in the Babel that is this seminar, we utter a word in one language but it can be heard in two, as in Psalm 61 (60)

JLN: Do you mean a half a work?

MCS: Rather an in-between-work...

JLN: Well, first specifically, I was asking what is *Demiurgos*?

MCS: The word comes from *demos*, as in democracy...

JLN: That is a bit odd ... *Demiurgos* ... [Nancy looks into his dictionary]. So... «Demiourgos is the man that works for the people.» There you are, you're right! Ah, but this is very interesting! It's beautiful!

MCS: Yes, but it depends on how one understands and hears the sense of *demos*. Is it necessary to understand *demos* from out of *ergon*, from the urgency of putting something in work or, on the contrary, should the urgency of the work be understood from *demos*? Or is this alternative inadequate? The difficulty, I think, lies in the demiurgical vocabulary, in the demiurgy of language itself because, in presenting the thesis of the demiurge, Plato succumbs to this very human vice of taking the gift and what is given by nature as a "fact", that is, as a work, an *oeuvre*. I am thinking here of some words of Valéry, who is surprised by this immediate translation of donation/gift to fact. He said: «I look for the first time at this thing found, I notice what I said regarding its form, and I am puzzled. That's when I wonder: Who made this? My first impulse was to think about the making. The idea of making is the first and most human one.» Why, when something happens to us, and when we feel the strange surprise of life itself, why do we ask the question about the "making" of the work? Why instead of just receiving, do we place ourselves in the perspective of having? Here is the genesis of the issue of causality that obliges to call its genesis a "craftwork", which explains in part why the words used by the *Demiurgos* are *cheiroplastés*, *tekton*... the manufacturer who produces things, entities. Of course the whole process of the life of beings is discussed here but the image is the one of hypostasis, of what is most visible. It is in this vision which replaces receiving with having that one immediately loses from view being in its becoming, but it is there, of course...

JLN: We lose it... But I myself would say that we do not [altogether] lose it, but that we lose it first when one separates the image in order to stay within its terrain. This is a good way, as you said earlier, of approaching exactly the question of ground, because we have this idea that is incredibly old and persistent in the Western tradition of thinking that there is the image on the one hand, but then behind it there is necessarily something else, some other thing which is its ground, at once the model, the manufacturer of the image, but also the material that subtends the image, the *subjectile* as we say in French – that is to say the material with which we do something: the canvas, the matter, the wood, the marble. Derrida has written a text on Artaud called *Forcener le subjectile*. So we have this habit, and this may be one of the biggest differences between our culture and perhaps all other cultures in the world (like the difference in relation to the subject of myth which we discussed yesterday), is that in all other cultures, the image is precisely the presentation of its own background. It resembles the Latin *imago* which also had another meaning signifying images of ancestors. But I believe that the images of ancestors were not intended to be representations, copies of the ancestor, a sort of human form, but they were rather said to be the grandfather or grandmother themselves, and these *imaginings* were first locked away in a sacred wardrobe in the house, the patrician having the right to take them out into the streets on certain holidays. There was a certain right known as *jus imaginum*, connected to the right to take out these images… This shows that the Latin *imago* was something very religious, if you want, a kind of magic: it was a presence, a presencing and not at all a representation. And I think that for us the images of art, of art in terms of image, mean precisely that; an image in which we do not look for a ground behind it. For example, if we take this picture [JLN shows a picture in an advertisement for an educational institution lying on the table] we understand that there is an intention behind the image, that someone has created this image, that it is illustrative, allegorical, because it shows the child, the child's culture, a child is playing, etc... Nothing is *in* the picture, everything is in what lies behind it, elsewhere. But if you take another picture, for example, *Agnus Dei*, the Lamb by Francisco de Zurbarán, then it is another matter. It is not the reproduction of the scene, but the scene itself – of course you can say whatever you want, for instance that it refers to the history of the Christian Lamb, which is a Jewish and Christian history, the New Testament, the Lamb of a sacrificed god, etc. But it is not that which is there: it is the painting itself in its extraordinary precision, this really is sheep's wool. This is much more a matter of the touch, and certainly not of the representation of the touch. It is a touching by and for the eye, it places the wool within the eye. So if we knew how to think the appearing of the world like that, that is to say, where everything is in appearing, in the sense I meant earlier of coming to appearing, then we do not in fact necessarily lose it, although, of course, it at the same time interrupts language, because one could say that it would become very difficult if I really wanted to speak about the sheep's wool, and gradually, it may become as difficult as speaking about music.

We talked yesterday with Peter about music. It is a very particular, and very interesting problem, the difficulty of speaking about music. There is a kind of line of oscillation here between three discourses, three kinds of speaking: the musicological discourse, the allegorical discourse and a non-discursive discourse of, and on, music. In Mozart's Clarinet Concerto, for instance, the clarinet is in dialogue with the orchestra, there is a love story between clarinet and orchestra, yes! it can be very, very exciting, even for the musicians to play, and I quote someone who is a very good musician, admirable, and who said during a rehearsal before a concert: «oh, you must hear this, it is a dialogue, it is a love story, or ... I do not know what, it is about jealousy, quarrel ...». So I said to myself, this is all very well for the musician, but the music *itself* is not there, because you can say all kinds of things – it is love, it is hate, etc. But even so, at the limit, there is a third aspect, I do not know very well what can we say, we can try to talk about pulse and impulse, about ascending and descending, about enveloping and developing: many things, but in the end, we listen to the music and then it's over. Or rather, there it begins ...

To page 74ff.

MCS: We might recall, here, the difference between the discourses about Greece and the beginning of philosophy in Husserl and in Heidegger. One big difference is that Husserl assumes that there is an original philosophical Greece which was lost in the modern world because of the naturalization of consciousness, etc., while for Heidegger the beginning of philosophy, is already the loss of philosophy. For him, the beginning is the loss.

JLN: But of course, Heidegger discusses the West as a beginning through a loss. The loss of the Pre-Socratic, the loss of the wonder of being, but later on he changes.

MCS: Maybe, but I think that what you have said is more decisive. If I understood you correctly, you wanted to remind us that it is important to leave this discursivity about loss and losses, in the sense of «oh, we can never return back», somehow in the sense discussed [yesterday] by the student from Turkey, (unfortunately not recorded) saying that this place at which you can never arrive, namely Greece, is more than a place to which we can never return, a place which we can never lose. It would also mean that there is no «loss of grounds», but that «ground» is at the same time ... what is the contrary of loss?

To page 79ff.

Beckett does not say it but he thinks it, and in order to say it he uses rather the word «reflux», as in the verse: «Encore le dernier reflux, le gallé mort, le demi tour puis le part vers la vieille lumière». In the text *Lessness*, the *without* – which for him is «meaning» – Beckett speaks neither of the «loss» nor of the «absence» of grounds – he speaks about becoming while in dissolution, he speaks, I think, about a *gerundive*, about a name, and the name is «unnameable.» My question would be whether the discourse on «loss of grounds», which is the title of our project, which has as its starting point the «absence of ground», the *Abgründigkeit*, would not remain hostage to a fundamentalism of being? Put differently, is there a difference between «loss», «absence» and the «without», the «Lessness»? It seems to me that «loss», «absence» always speaks «after» the foundation, «after» the subject, «after» the wall, and that these expressions produce an «after-ism» that reinforces the logic of fundament and foundations, the foundational logic that covers up the meaning of thrown existence as existence without reasons to exist. In the «after-ism» of a discourse about «loss» and «absence», the question about «what to do then?», «what should be done?» is constantly reproduced. But in the «without», glimpsed by Beckett, it seems that the non-way out of existence shows the reflux of existence, shows existence as reflux, as becoming while in dissolution, a «*ruisseau qu'on devine à peine*», a small opening that is almost a small *clarière*, clearing, »chimera, light », something that I think you are thinking all the time, but that sounds clearer to me when you named *entre-être*, between-being, I think.

To page 97ff.

Time and memory are probably the main elements related to a musician's thinking, if we can call it a thought or rather an active itinerary to dissolve presence. For a musician, thoughts circulate around the present time in the search for a more ethereal relation to absence. One may wonder if memory remembers absence or presence. Can memory have a remembrance of memory? An answer to this question can only be found in listening to where all these parameters coincide and dissolve simultaneously by their own existence. The listening to absences is what enables us to listen to presences. My piece *Absence* from 1975 was written to work out this issue. The title as well as the contents concern the circuits of memory: the memory of what we have listened to and the memory of that to which we know we will listen. We find countless sound events. In the absence, a presence emerges. The relationship between the two provides an extension of the memory of absence and the shortening of memory in the present. Perhaps it is here that music shows most clearly the gap between the writing and the performing of a particular given at every instant, of the improvised. In improvisation, it just happens that memory reminds us of what is to come and makes us leave the past for the sake of the presence of absence.

Regarding the visit to Jean-Luc Nancy at Strasbourg, I did not come as a member of the research group but only as a follower. It was important and somehow right for me to stay apart from the academic discussions, which certainly gave me much joy. Memory seemed to me all the time to be at the center of all that I heard. It was as much memory of the future as memory of the past. So I was both absent and present.

On the last day, when the group met at Jean-Luc Nancy's home, whom I had already met in Saint Petersburg, where we spent two days together, he asked me a question about music and the reading of scores. My answer seemed to surprise him because I said that in looking at a score, the musician sees rather than listens to it. With this question I find it impossible not to participate in the general discussion. But as the discussion slowly changed course, it faded gradually. Presence through absence.

My piece *Absence* deals with the memory of a time, memory as much of the absence as of the presence, with the memory of improvisation. As an instrument I chose the viola, which most expresses loneliness. In its construction, it is the closest to my instrument, the cello, but in its spirit it is maybe the most distant. In fact, it is only in proximity that absence can develop. The piece is for me today as a notebook of memories of a time that was revealed to me again through this visit to Jean-Luc Nancy. The piece was therefore remade by his presence.

To page 100

Exposed on the mountains of the heart. See, how small there,
see: the last hamlet of words, and higher.
and yet so small, a last
homestead of feeling. Do you recognize it?
Exposed on the mountains of the heart. Rocky earth
under the hands. But something will
flower here; out of the mute abyss
flowers and unknowing herb in song.
But the knowing? Ah, that you who began to understand
and are silent now, exposed on the mountains of the heart.
Yet many as awareness still whole wanders there,
many a self-confident moutain animal
passes through and remains. And that great protected bird
circles about the peaks of pure denial, but
unprotected, here on the mountains of the heart.

www.ingramcontent.com/pod-product-compliance
Lightning Source LLC
Chambersburg PA
CBHW020249010526
44107CB00002B/172